AF619523

1939-1945
WORLD WAR TWO

AUTHOR

Paolo Crippa (23 April 1978) has cultivated his passion for Italian history since high school. His research interests are focused mainly in the field of military history and in particular on italian armored units from the 30s until the end of World War II. In 2006 he published his first volume, *"I Reparti Corazzati della Repubblica Sociale Italiana 1943/1945"*, the first organic research carried out and published in Italy on the subject. In 2007 he published *"Duecento Volti della R.S.I."* and in 2011 *" Un anno con il 27° Reggimento Artiglieria Legnano"*. He regularly contributes to several journals: Milites, New Historica, SGM - World War II, Batailes & Blindes, Armoured Vehicles and history of the twentieth century, Mezzi Corazzati, both as an author, or in collaboration with other researchers. He published with the editor Mattioli 1885 in 2014 *"Italy 43 - 45 - Civil War improvised AFV's"* (2014), *"Italian AFV's of the Civil War 1943 - 1945"* (2015) and *"Italy 43 - 45 - AFV's and MV's of co-belligerent units"* (2018).

PUBLISHING'S NOTES

LICENSES COMMONS

For a complete list of Soldiershop titles please contact Luca Cristini Editore on our website: www.soldiershop.com or www.cristinieditore.com. E-mail: info@soldiershop.com

Title: **THE ARMORED UNITS OF THE ROYAL ARMY AND THE ARMISTICE VOL. 2** Code.: **WTW-024 EN**
by Paolo Crippa ISBN code: 978-88-93277563 First edition may 2021
Text: English Nr. of images: 102 layout: 177,8x254mm Cover & Art Design: Luca S. Cristini

WITNESS TO WAR (SOLDIERSHOP) is a trademark of Luca Cristini Editore, via Orio, 35/4 - 24050 Zanica (BG) ITALY.

WITNESS TO WAR

THE ARMORED UNITS OF THE ROYAL ARMY AND THE ARMISTICE VOL. 2

PHOTOS & IMAGES FROM WORLD WARTIME ARCHIVES

PAOLO CRIPPA

BOOKS TO COLLECT

SUMMARY

INTRODUCTION

After having described, in the previous volume, the fighting in Rome between 8 and 10 September 1943, which led to the loss of the capital, in the following pages the events that occurred in the city after the cessation of hostilities will be reviewed: the rapid disarmament of the "Piave" Division, which had been entrusted with the control of public order and the transfer of public security functions to the Italian African Police, which operated, even with its armored vehicles, until the arrival of the Americans on June 4, 1944.

The heroic episodes of Resistance that occurred in the rest of the Peninsula will be recalled later, of which the armored units were protagonists, in Piombino, Parma, Piacenza and Sardinia, as well as what happened to the armored units outside the national borders in Dalmatia, Albania, in the Aegean, in Corsica. The text will conclude with the discussion of the (failed) attempts to reconstitute armored units within the Royal Co-belligerent Army and the contribution made by the Tankers to the liberation struggle.

As always, I approach every new research work with enthusiasm and with respect for the events (and above all the people, actors on the stage of History) that I will talk about. But to complete any study this is not enough, documents are not enough, but the contribution that many friends bring, each to a different extent, but all equally valuable, is needed. I would therefore like to remember, in an absolutely random order, Lorenzo Tonioli, Luigi Manes, Antonio Tallillo and Ralph Ricco, who "went hunting" for photographs from their archives, news, documents, books.

Giovanni and Agostina D'Alessandro also provided pictures of their father, who had fought in Sardinia in the crucial months of 1943. I would also like to thank Colonel Maurizio Parri, who shared memories and photographs of the experience of his father Raffaello, a young officer of the 4th Tank Regiment in Rome and active member of the Resistance in the capital. An important thanks to my friend Niccolò Tognarini, whose fundamental contribution was used to reconstruct the events that took place in Piombino between 8 and 10 September 1943, thanks to the generous documentation made available, documentation from the archive of his father Professor Ivano, who for years studied the subject with great passion and whose research work earned him the award of the Gold Medal for Military Valor to the Banner of the Municipality of the Tuscan city for these episodes. I cannot forget the now late Nino Arena and Giorgio Pisanò, who generously opened their archives to me.

And finally, thanks to Fabio D 'Inzeo, officer of the Cavalry Army, who" went ahead "in September 2020, for the many news he shared with me over many years of friendship. I dedicate this work to him, happy to have met him and to have had him as a friend, united by the passion for history and model making: we spent many pleasant moments together.

Thank you all!
The author

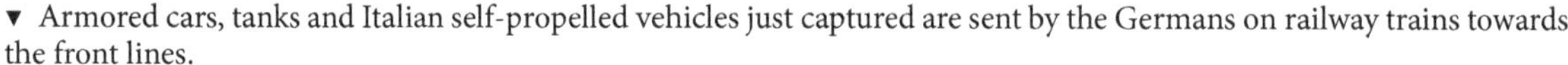

▲ An AB41 armored car of the Motorcycle Armored Corps loaded on a railway platform ready to be used by the German armed forces.

▼ Armored cars, tanks and Italian self-propelled vehicles just captured are sent by the Germans on railway trains towards the front lines.

ROME AFTER THE CAPITULATION

After the signing of the surrender of the Italian armed forces on 10 September, the dissolution of the armed units and the establishment of the "Open City" of Rome, as we saw in the previous volume, the Germans maintained a public order service, guaranteed by Italian military. The "Piave" Division was the only large unit not to be obliged to hand over their arms and to be dissolved. The German military leaders in fact destined it to be used as a unit that was to guarantee order in the capital, probably to give the population the impression of a gradual passage of competences and not of a lightning occupation. The "Piave" Division, under the command of Brigadier General Ugo Tabellini, was therefore reorganized, deprived of heavy armament and placed under the orders of the Command of the Open City of Rome. Next to the "Piave" the structure of the Italian African Police was maintained, which was not deprived even of the armored vehicles at its disposal, to the detriment of the Carabinieri, considered by the Germans too close to the reigning House of Savoy and therefore not reliable. . In the days following the Italian surrender, a dozen AS42 vans of the Motorized Assault Battalion (and their crews) were absorbed by the PAI, to prevent them from being seized by the Germans, and a new company was thus established, the 13th, commanded by the Captain Roberto Curcio, also from the Motorized Assault Battalion.

On the other hand, about 300 volunteers of the Arditi Truckers, coming from the 112th Truckers Company of the II Battalion of the X, commanded by Captain Paolo Paris, and by the 133rd Company (formed almost entirely by veterans of the "Young Fascists" Regiment), but also by other soldiers from the newly formed "Cyclone" Paratroopers Division, came into contact with the 2.Fallshirmjäger-Division "Ramke" and managed to get three members of the unit accepted. The Italian military was divided into two groups and one of these, under the command of Captain Paris, was aggregated to the German Division as an Exploring Group, equipped with some AS42 Metropolitane[1]. The "Paris" Group, as it will later be known, worked for a few days to guarantee the radio broadcasts of the EIAR and, after a short training period, the Truckers followed the 2.Fallshirmjäger-Division in Ukraine at the end of October. The unit took part in the harsh clashes sustained dalla "Ramke", suffering numerous human losses, including the commander Captain Paris himself; all the vans were lost during the winter, the last ones during the retreat to Romania in spring 1944.

The strange situation created in Rome, with the presence of an entire Italian Division appointed to guarantee order, lasted a few days: on 23 September, in fact, following the declaration of the birth of the Italian Social Republic, generals Calvi di Bergolo, Tabellini and Maraffa (commander in chief of the PAI) were suddenly arrested. The buildings of the "Giulio Cesare" and "Ugo Bartolomei" schools in the Nomentano and Africano districts, where the Regiments of the "Piave" were based, were quickly surrounded by the paratroopers of the VII Regiment of the 2. Fallschirmjäger-Division, the Italian soldiers were disarmed and sent to places of detention, while all the materials of the Division were confiscated by the Germanic armed forces and the Division effectively dissolved.

From that date, therefore, the PAI, under the command of General Umberto Presti, remained the only Italian armed unit, together with the reconstituted Police, to garrison Rome with the consent of the Germans, and kept the armored-armored vehicles supplied in perfect efficiency. , which were used for institutional services. The Italian African Police, became the Police Force of the "Open City" of Rome, was headquartered in the "Mussolini" Forum, and its commander, liked by the Germans, managed to weave relations with the anti-fascists and the Roman Resistance. The department continued to carry out its police functions throughout the period of the German occupation of the

1 Sources disagree on the number of AS42 vans used by the "Paris", from a minimum of 6 to a maximum of 9.

capital, refusing to replace the stars on the collar with fasces, despite the fact that specific rules had been issued to this effect[2].

In circumstances not fully clarified, an AS42 Metropolitana van of the P.A.I. it was literally destroyed by fire from an American tank on June 4, 1944 in via Nazionale. Upon the arrival of the allies in the capital, the 13th Company of the "Cheren" Column was charged with moving the P.A.I. located in the city, concentrating them at the Ministry of War, to prevent them from falling into the hands of the German troops and the R.S.I. in retreat. During the transfer, the soldiers of the P.A.I. they clashed several times with German and Fascist soldiers, a circumstance that forced the last three vans of the column to change their route, towards Via Nazionale. Before reaching it, the crews of the P.A.I. again had to open fire with the onboard machine guns against a German barrage and, having overcome the last obstacle, the van commanded by Lieutenant Carlo Pettini, with 5 other guards on board, entered via Nazionale at the same time as the US avant-gardes were going up from the Termini Station area, coming from Via Casilina. The Americans, having just heard the gunshots coming from the side street and believing they were therefore under enemy attack, hit Pettini's truck in full with a precise 75 mm cannon shot, exploded by a Sherman tank , who gutted the vehicle and killed the entire crew. In addition to Lieutenant Carlo Pettini, the auxiliary guards of the P.A.I. Romeo Aureli, Francesco Bucchieri, Savino De Ponzio, Angelo Perotti and Michele Puddu[3].

Upon the arrival of the Allies, the departments of the Italian African Police present in Rome disbanded in an orderly fashion, handing over their vehicles to the police, including at least 11 AS42 Metropolitana. The Rome Police Headquarters, in fact, had already established a Mobile Battalion of Public Security since 1938, which was based at the barracks of the Forte Tiburtino. The Battalion, in which some Tankers of the 4th Regiment had also converged, after the dissolution of the department following the clashes of September 1943, had an Armored Company with L3 tanks and AB41 armored cars, material that was reinforced with of the AS42 vans of the Metropolitan model of the dissolved PAI, armored vehicles that were used to carry out public order services.

---

2 The P.A.I. resisted any attempt at interference by the authorities of the Social Republic and even when an attempt was made to reorganize its structure, with the opening of the school in Busto Arsizio (VA) in the autumn of 1943 (to bring the PAI at the heart of CSR) and with its incorporation into the GNR, the colonial police force managed to maintain a strong autonomy, so much so that the Command remained in Rome until the arrival of the Anglo-Americans.

3 In this regard, see "Polizia dell'Africa Italian (1937-1945)" by Piero Crociani (work cited in the bibliography). However, there are other versions of the episode. A report by Captain Curcio, which substantially confirms the thesis set out in the text, states that Pettini's truck was chasing a German vehicle when it collided, by chance, with an American tank. In contrast to this version, in a communication from the Command of the Royal Carabinieri of Rome, classified as "Personal confidential", addressed to the Minister of the Interior and dated May 19, 1945, with the subject "Arrest of informers", regarding the Lieutenant Pettini, we read: "Bettini [in this way in the text!] was killed in Rome when the allied troops entered, while with others he tried to hinder the advance of the Anglo-American avant-gardes". According to what is reported in this statement, therefore, the truck was sustaining a clash with the American units and was therefore not accidentally hit. This other version was taken up by Benedetto Pafi and Bruno Benvenuti in their "Rome at War - unpublished images September 1943-June 1944" (work cited in the bibliography): the two authors argue that Lieutenant Pettini's vehicle was the last truck firing at the Americans on June 4, 1944. Finally, Nicola Pignato and Filippo Cappellano "The combat vehicles of the Italian Army", volume II, work cited in the bibliography) move the event to June 6, to liberate the city by now completed, when, according to this version, 2 PAI vans they were on patrol, one in Piazza di Spagna and the other on the corner of via XXIV Maggio and via Nazionale. The second vehicle, whose crew would have been composed of 2 officers and 4 guards, would have been destroyed, after having crossed a US tank, before the second truck arrived.

▲ The officers of the General Staff of the Motorcycle Armored Corps preside over the delivery of the approximately 350 Italian armored vehicles concentrated in the plain of Ponte Lucano in Bagni di Tivoli on 13 September 1943. In the center, Colonel Menotti Chieli, who represents the Italian side in the delivery of materials, to his left the Chief of Staff of the "Ariete II" Division, Colonel Carlo Salinari. The Germans inventoried all the requisite material (Arena) with meticulous meticulousness.

▼ Armored vehicles and vehicles of the "Lancers of Vittorio Emanuele II" regiment piled up in the area of Bagni di Tivoli, waiting to be picked up by the German units (Arena).

▲ Two German paratroopers stand guard over the tanks and self-propelled vehicles of the "Lancers of Vittorio Emanuele II": the vehicles were all in perfect operating conditions. In the foreground, on the right, there is a control wagon for self-propelled batteries (Arena).

▼ Tanks M15 / 42 of the "Lancers of Vittorio Emanuele II" Regiment waiting to be taken over by Germanic units (Arena).

▲ On 13 September, units of the 2. Fallschirmjäger-Division approached the 136th Armored Division "Centauro II" to proceed with the disarmament of the large Italian unit. After the fall of Mussolini, the soldiers of the "M" Armored Division were replaced with the bands at the collar with the royal stars and gray-green sachets were distributed in place of the black fezes, evident changes in this image (BA).

▼ After the fighting in the capital, the soldiers of the "Piave" Division, deprived of heavy weapons, and the soldiers of the Italian African Police were charged with maintaining public order in the city of Rome, in a strange climate of collaboration with the Germanic armed forces, which had set up numerous checkpoints on the streets, also supported by artillery pieces (BA).

▲ In the courtyard of what used to be the barracks of the Legion Allievi Carabinieri "Legnano" in Rome, on 12 September Major Gericke decorated with the Iron Cross his paratroopers from his Battalion, who had distinguished themselves during the assault on the Headquarters of the Royal Army of Centro Marte in Monterotondo. Behind the deployed Fallschirmjäger unit are parked several self-propelled 75/18 M42 units captured by the Italian units during the clashes in the capital (B.A.).

▼ An AS42 Camionetta Metropolitana of the 10th Arditi Regiment surrounded by German paratroopers on 18 September 1943, when about 300 soldiers of the Regiment, reached the capital, managed to join the 2.Fallshirmjäger-Division "Ramke". It is probably a command vehicle, because it is armed only with an 8 mm machine gun, the photo also highlights the camouflage color of the vehicle and the "RE 1192B" plate. On the hood of the car, above the spare wheel housing, a large painting with a photograph of Mussolini was placed.

▲ A second lieutenant of the 10th Arditi Regiment discusses with an officer and some German paratroopers of the 2.Fallshirmjäger-Division "Ramke". The Italian officer wears the characteristic magazine pouch called "Samurai" and at the collar of the jacket you can see the two-pointed blue flames of the Arditi.

▼ In the capital, two M tanks of the reconstituted "Leonessa" Group, driven by tankers wearing black shirts again, guard Palazzo Wedekind in Piazza Colonna, where the Roman Fascio was reconstituted between 17 and 18 September. The tanks belonged to the 3rd Tank Regiment and had arrived in Rome shortly before the Armistice to arm the IX Tank Battalion being rebuilt, at the depot of the 4th Tank Regiment (Crippa).

▲ Two AB41s and two motorcyclists from the Italian African Police guard Piazza Venezia in Rome in the days following the capitulation of the Italian armed forces. The P.A.I., at the request of the German authorities, remained in arms and continued to guarantee public order in the capital until the arrival of the Anglo-Americans in June 1944.

▼ Without any warning, on 23 September 1943, the German command ordered to disarm the "Piave" Division, which was in charge of garrisoning Rome (B.A.)

▲ The paratroopers of the 2.Fallschirmjäger-Division surround the "Giulio Cesare" Institute where part of the "Piave" Division is headquartered, to proceed with the disarmament.

▼ The disarmament of the Italians of the "Piave" Motorized Division begins in the courtyard of the "Giulio Cesare" high school, in Corso Trieste: the officers hand over their guns.

▲ The individual and team weapons of the soldiers of the "Piave" are stacked by soldiers of the Feldgendarmerie, while the trucks of the Division are thoroughly inspected.

▲ Without any unnecessary resistance being attempted, the Fallschirmjäger frame the unarmed Italian soldiers rounded up in the "Ugo Bartolomei" school.

▼ German paratroopers armed with machine guns guard the numerous vehicles requisitioned from the "Piave" Division (B.A.).

▲ Soldiers of the "Piave" Division, guarded by a group of German paratroopers, await their fate, probably in via Bressanone.

▼ It is the end also for the "Piave" Division: the Italian soldiers, aboard the same trucks requisitioned the unit, are sent to concentration and detention places.

▲ L3 tanks of the Mobile Battalion of the Rome Police in the spring of 1944: you can see the camouflage and the emblem of the Police on the wagon in the foreground. Many men and vehicles came from the 4th Tank Regiment (Parri).

▼ Tankers of the dissolved 4th Tank Infantry Regiment aggregated to the Mobile Battalion of Public Security in Rome, photographed in the spring of 1944. In the center, with the bag, Lieutenant Raffaello Parri, distinguished in the clashes at Porta San Paolo, who joined the clandestine formations soldiers of the Roman Resistance (Parri).

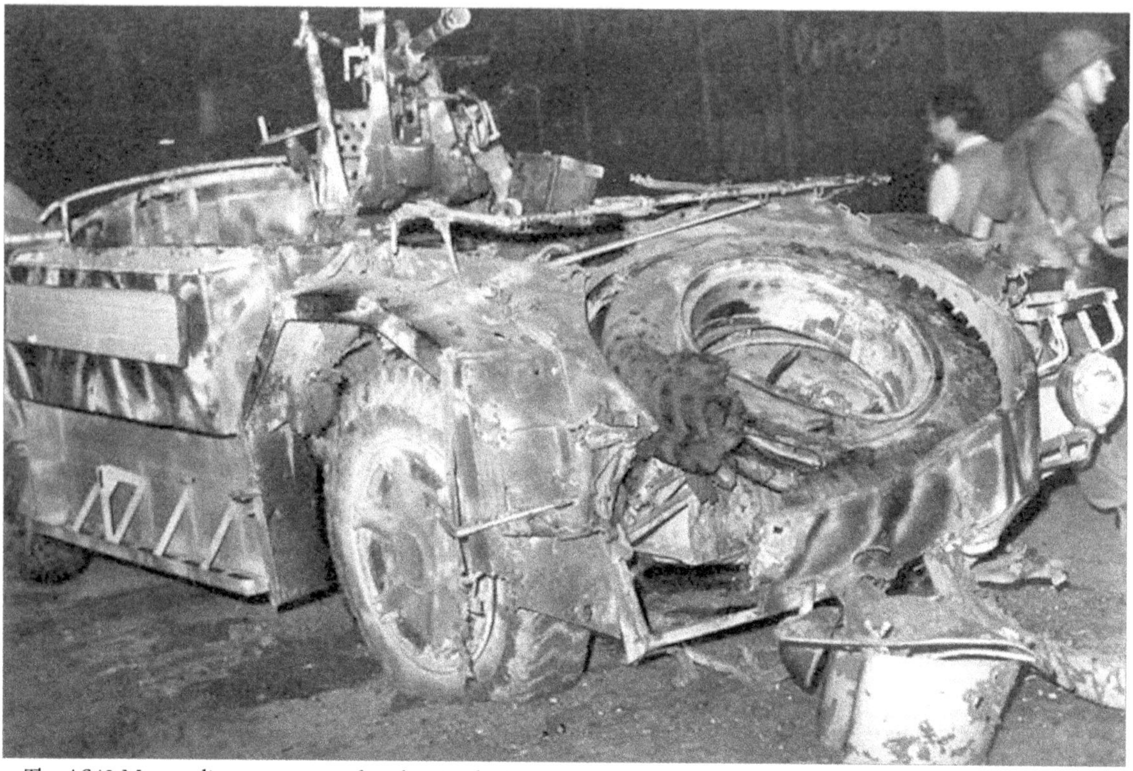

▲ The AS42 Metropolitana van, armed with a Breda 20 mm machine gun and an 8 mm machine gun, belonging to the Lieutenant of the P.A.I. Carlo Pettini, destroyed on 4 June 1944 in Via Nazionale in Rome by a cannon shot, fired from an American tank.

▼ The next morning, the destroyed vehicle of the Italian African Police is observed with curiosity by passers-by.

▲ The Auxiliary Lieutenant of the 13th Company of the "Cheren" Column of the Italian African Police Carlo Pettini, who died on June 4, 1944 aboard the AS42 truck he commanded.

▲ An AS42 Metropolitana truck of the P.A.I. through the streets of the capital on 4 or 5 June 1944: the tricolor flag was probably used to avoid being mistaken for a German vehicle as happened with Lieutenant Pettini's vehicle.

▼ Elements of the Mobile Public Security Battalion in front of the Roman prison of Regina Coeli during a revolt of the prisoners. The policemen are supported by some L3 wagons and by an AS42 truck (Crippa).

▲ An AB41 armored car of the Mobile Public Security Battalion in via San Francesco di Sales, along the perimeter of the Roman prison, ready to intervene. The symbol in the turret is interesting, representing an ace of spades (Crippa).

▼ Police officers around a Camionetta Metropolitana, ready to intervene against the rioting inmates. The vehicle is armed with a Breda 20mm machine gun (Crippa).

▲ Another AS42 Subway truck in command version, that is, without heavy armament, labeled "POLIZIA 255", from the rapid department of the Rome Police during the same prison revolt. These vans were sold to the Mobile Public Security Battalion by the P.A.I., after the dissolution following the arrival of the Americans in the capital (Crippa).

▼ American soldiers inspect the L6 / 40 tanks of the Italian African Police after their entry into the city. The image allows you to appreciate the sand yellow color of the tanks and the presence of the back "PAI", without numbering, painted on the bow.

THE REACTION OF THE ARMORED UNITS IN THE REST OF THE PENINSULA

The fighting in Rome in September 1943 is rightly considered one of the first acts of the Italian military reaction against the Germans, who suddenly passed from allies to enemies. The fact that a large number of departments and units took part in the clashes in Rome, varying in size and specialty, together with the symbolic value of the defense of the capital, mean that this episode was taken as a symbol of the Italian military resistance.

No less important, however, were the responses to the first hostile acts carried out by the Germanic armed forces in other cities of Italy, some of which operated by armored units, which unanimously chose to sacrifice men and means in an attempt to stem the German aggressions, such as act of courage and response to the tragic circumstances of the Armistice.

Whole departments sacrificed themselves, literally fired up to the last bullet before accepting defeat, resulting in truly heavy human losses, challenging the opponent beyond any reasonable limit. Let us therefore also retrace these acts of heroism, which took place in Piombino, Parma, Piacenza, Sardinia.

1. Piombino

The Tuscan coastal town, in the province of Livorno, became the protagonist of an important act of revolt against the Germans in the days immediately following the Armistice[4], in which the XIX Tank Battalion also took part, commanded by Lieutenant Colonel Angelo Falcone, who was dependent on the 31st Regiment of Siena. The Battalion, mobilized on April 22, 1943, was initially intended for North Africa, as a basin to feed the 133rd Tank Regiment of the "Littorio" Division, and the completion of its staff was slow due to the lack of armored vehicles. so much so that the department reached full training practically only in the middle of 1943[5], with this structure:

- Command
- Comando Company, under the command of Captain Marcello Bidinost
- 1st M15/42 Tank Company , under the command of Captain Di Gregorio, on 20 wagons, not all equipped with anti-aircraft guns
- 2nd Self-propelled 75/34 M42 Company
- 3rd Self-propelled 75/34 M42 Company

The Battalion had a staff of 22 officers and 434 between non-commissioned officers and troops and an availability of 20 M15 / 42 tanks and 18 self-propelled 75/34 M42[6], some of which are still running in, divided between the two Self-propelled Companies. Each Self-propelled Company was divided into:

- Squad Command, with 1 self-propelled for the squad commander

4 It is worth pointing out that Piombino was already in turmoil since 25 July. With the fall of Mussolini, in fact, a ferment had been created in the city among the workers of the metalworking companies, ferment fomented by a group of communists who operated in hiding among the workers. The city, thanks to the presence of important factories and the port, which made it possible to connect Sardinia and Corsica with peninsular Italy, was a very important strategic objective for the Germanic armed forces.
5 The M15 / 42 tanks were delivered to the Battalion practically immediately after the mobilization, while the assignment of the self-propelled vehicles proceeded with the dropper.
6 Some sources incorrectly indicate that they were 75/18 self-propelled.

- 1st Self-Propelled Platoon, on 4 pieces
- 2nd Self-Propelled Platoon, on 4 pieces

After following a period of training in Colle Val d'Elsa and San Gimignano, the Battalion was assigned on 5 July 1943 to the Territorial Defense Command of Florence, which assigned it to the defense of the Piombino sector. The XIXth then moved to the destination area, placed only operationally dependent on the 215th Coastal Division, and took up position in the Rimigliano pine forest in Torrenuova, between the Via Aurelia and the Via Piombinese, about 11 km from Piombino, with the Carri Company M in the city with tasks of public order. On 1 September the XIX Battalion was assigned, as we have seen in the previous volume, to the 136th Armored Division "Centauro II" (formerly the 1st Armored Division "M"), but the unit never reached its destination. The Battalion was operational only on paper: there was no ammunition (only 105 shots were available for the 47/40 guns of the M tanks, while the self-propelled ones were completely devoid of bullets, a problem repeatedly reported to the higher commands) and the fuel was scarce. A few days before 8 September it was possible to requisition part of the cargo of a railway train, which had been stationary for days at the Campiglia Marittima station, thus creating a minimum supply of fuel.

The day after the announcement of the Armistice, in the early hours of the day, there was the first clashes between Germans and Italians in Portovecchio. On the same day the XIX Tank Battalion received the order to take 2,000 grenade bags of 47/40 and 3,000 of 75/34 from the Valle Ugione Artillery Depot in Stagno (LI) and, for this reason, an officer was sent with a truck launches 3RO equipped with a trailer, which however had to return empty-handed, because the warehouse was without ammunition, so much so that a written declaration was issued to the tanker officer, attesting to this pernicious situation[7]. In the afternoon, under the orders of General Perni, the XIX Battalion moved about 5 km from Piombino, to block all access roads from the sea to the city; the order also gave instructions to destroy all confidential and secret documents of the department and to oppose any German initiative, but not to oppose any possible allied landing[8]. On the following night between 9 and 10 September two German torpedo boats docked in Portovecchio, with the excuse of requesting a supply of water and fuel; the German sailors landed, taking advantage of the behavior of the Italian soldiers, who wanted to avoid any clash, occupied some positions of the Royal Navy[9]. In the following hours, a steamer and some landing units also entered the port, some of which headed for the industrial area, evidently with the aim of occupying the city. At that point the Piombinese population began to mobilize, giving a hand to the soldiers of the coastal batteries[10], while around 16:00 the Commander of Piazza Generale Perni gave the order to the XIX Battalion to come in force to Piombino, settling in Piazza Vittorio Emanuele, arranging the armored vehicles along Corso Italia. This order, if on the one hand it appeared as an act aimed at defending the city from German attacks, on the other it was certainly a maneuver by General Perni to try to restore order in the city, where the initiative of the civil insurgents was going to fill that void of authority that was gradually

7 The withdrawal order was issued simultaneously by both the 31st Tank Regiment Command and the Piombino Sector Command.

8 This last order was issued directly by Superesercito.

9 Part of the battery sailors had left their posts unguarded to concentrate at the train station, hoping to be able to catch a train back home. In the middle of the morning groups of workers, who had obtained the weapons abandoned by the soldiers of the anti-aircraft batteries, who had in turn moved away from the pieces, tried to convince the sailors to return to their positions, to try to strike up a resistance against the Germans.

10 The participation of civilians in the so-called "battle of Piombino" was massive. The population violently demonstrated against the Germans and worked to rebuild the staff of the batteries and artillery positions, also giving support to the XIX Tank Battalion during the clashes with armed squads. The anti-fascist committee, which led the civilian insurgents, managed to give an orderly direction to the reaction of the Italian Armed Forces, which initially had disbanded in a worrying way.

being created[11]. At 6:00 pm on September 10, the 19th Battalion finally reached the city, greeted by a crowd of cheering citizens. The Command Company, the 2nd and the 3rd Company assumed the planned positions, while 2 self-propelled vehicles of the 2nd Company, under the command of Major Cimino, were sent to the ILVA industrial plant and another 2 in support of the 1st Company, deployed in defense between the city and the port (2 Platoons in defense of the port, the others in defense of the town), to block the way to possible German attacks[12]. The M15 wagons, stationed as the first line of defense in via Antonio Pacinotti, were in a favorable position which made them invisible from the sea, but which still allowed them to beat the coast with the weapons on board, while the self-propelled ones were placed on a chessboard in the transversal streets of the town, camouflaged between the buildings. A Company of the LVI Coastal Battalion was deployed to reinforce the XIX M Tank Battalion. Finally, Captain Di Gregorio deployed with 3 M and 2 self-propelled tanks near the headquarters of the Sector Command, as a reserve force. Around 9:30 pm a fire fight began between some German ships and the Italian coastal positions and, during the night, the machine guns of the M tanks often fired at German patrols, which tried to approach the industrial area. At 1:00 am on the 11th, the Piazza Command ordered a round-up of the entire port area, an operation that started only at 6 am, with the aim of pushing all the German soldiers towards the port docks. A group of 3 M tanks of the XIX Battalion supported a Platoon of the LVI Coastal Battalion, advancing on the main road, without finding a great resistance, while other M tanks had to clash with the Germans at Tolla Bassa to prevent infiltration into the ILVA Docks, managing to flush out all the Germans who had occupied the area (even infiltrating the positions of the same tanks), overcoming any form of resistance, but at the same time running out of scarce ammunition. The Germanic soldiers began to retreat, followed by the Italian tanks, which reached the port square around 8:30. Shortly after the German commander, requested a truce, obtained to be able to re-embark and leave the port by 11:30. Lieutenant Colonel Angelo Falcone had 6 tanks and 2 self-propelled tanks lined up on the port square, to keep the German embarkation operations under control. Around 17:00, after having collected their wounded, but without having suffered losses, the XIX Tank Battalion withdrew towards their camp, leaving two Platoons of the Carri M Company to guard the city.

Shortly before midnight, however, the commander of the 19th Tank Battalion received the order from the Piazza Command to bring the entire unit to the city in Porto Baratti, to hand over his vehicles and weapons to the Germanic units. After consulting his subordinates and informing the Piazza Command not to accept this provision, Lieutenant Colonel Falconi learned that the two Platoons who remained in Piombino had also received the same order and that the crews had abandoned the wagons, after having sabotaged them. Falconi, given the general state of disarray that was spreading among the departments of the Royal Army, firm in the intention not to deliver the wagons to the Germans and not to dissolve the department, therefore decided to have the Battalion queued in the direction of the Aurelia State Road, to head towards Siena. Here was the depot of the 31st Tank Regiment, where Lieutenant Colonel Falconi thought of making himself available to the commander, Colonel Formenti. Medical Lieutenant Monaci was sent on an advance, with a car and a truck, on which the wounded had been loaded, who had to contact the Regimental Command to request orders. On the morning of September 12, at 10, the rest of the XIX Battalion lined up for Siena; the

11 In Piombino, probably at the disposal of the 215th Coastal Division and to protect the Piazza Command in the city, there were also two L tanks, which, although present at the events of September 1943, did not take part in the battle.

12 According to the testimony of the Kapitänleutnant Albrand, commander of the destroyer ship TA11 and of the German convoy, the tanks of the XIX Battalion, once arrived in the city, were even used by General Perni, to try to disperse, by firing warning shots, the popular demonstration. , who clamored to intervene against the Germanic units: *"In the afternoon shots were heard coming from the city. Civilians were demonstrating. The Italian General warned me not to give weight to these shots. It was his tanks that fired on civilians. My sentries from the signal post confirmed this fact to me (...). Between 7.30pm and 8.30pm I learned, through rumors from the steel mills, that Italian troops and civilians too had intended to attack"* (BundesArchiv-MilitarArchiv Freiburg, Bestand: R.M.94/V./III M.124, papers 3-19).

column was made up of 4 M15 / 42 wagons, 18 self-propelled and 19 motor vehicles. 21 officers and 392 non-commissioned officers and enlisted men were counted on the appeal. Before Monterotondo Marittimo (GR) two M15 / 42s were abandoned, due to engine failures, caused by the ground not very favorable to the movement of armored vehicles, which had to move on their own tracks, since the Battalion had never received the wagon-carrying trolleys. In the afternoon, during the march, Lieutenant Monaci arrived directly from the regimental command, with the order of Colonel Formenti to abandon the wagons, after having made them unusable, given the absence of indications from the superior commands and given the danger of encountering units along the road to Siena. Lieutenant Colonel Falconi decided not to follow up on orders and made the column resume its march, after having had to abandon the other two M and two self-propelled wagons. At 6 pm the Battalion arrived in the locality of Montieri (GR), where, reached by the false news of the approach of a German unit, some tankmen, panicked, tried to flee. Falconi was forced to abandon all armored vehicles and decided to divide the Battalion on two columns, using only vehicles, one that should have aimed at San Giminiano and the second at Colle Val D'Elsa, before rejoining Siena. The two units set off in the course of the night and, the next morning, the first, arrived in San Giminiano, hiding its trucks, handed over its weapons to a German vanguard, which had arrived in the country. The second part of the Battalion found Colle Val D'Elsa occupied by Germanic units, to which it surrendered. Lieutenant Colonel Falconi declared the 19th M Tank Battalion dissolved on September 14, 1943.

In conclusion, we report the testimony of Lieutenant Filograno, of the XIX Tank Battalion, on the events of Piombino: "*I was in Piombino at the XIX Btg Carri M of the 31st Reg. Carristi, detached there, when the armistice was declared. The square in Piombino was commanded by Exc. Cesare M. De Vecchi and in the subordinate order there was another General. On the 9th, the Btg was used to reinforce the coastal departments. The Germans immediately occupied the port and the ironworks of Piombino and disarmed the military and dismissed the workers temporarily. In port there were two German fighters, an oil tanker and 7 or 8 barges. Some bourgeois took the batteries left by the military and opened fire on the Germans, who responded with the artillery of the fighters. On the evening of the 10th the Btg Carristi was assembled in Piombino and shortly afterwards the cannonade began between our batteries served by the bourgeois and sailors, our tanks against the German fighters and barges. In the morning we took prisoners the Germans guarding the railway and those of the damaged fighters and sunken boats* "[13].

2. Parma[14]

Parma was the seat of the 33rd Tank Infantry Regiment, a department intended for training and training tank personnel, commanded by Colonel Ugo Boldrini. At the date of the Armistice, the Regiment was almost completely devoid of tanks, as it had sent some operational departments to Corsica, with most of the armored vehicles available. Furthermore, after Mussolini's arrest, he had posted some platoons, with most of the few remaining tanks, to Milan, Piacenza and Reggio Emilia[15], to whom public order tasks were entrusted. In Parma itself, the 33rd Carristi had been called to garrison some hotspots in the city on 26 July. In particular, a unit on foot of the Regiment was sent to the city prison, where a procession of citizens, led by some Communist exponents, protested

13 Testimony reported by Professor Tognarini Ivano in his research "Documentazione per la Medaglia d'Oro", work cited in the bibliography, page 89.

14 For the drafting of this chapter, the primary source of information is the valuable research work of Mario Zannoni "Parma 1943, 8 settembre", work cited in the bibliography.

15 The news of the sending of departments to Reggio Emilia is reported in a report by the commander of the Regiment himself, Colonel Boldrini.

vehemently, demanding the release of political prisoners. Two M13 / 40 tanks of the Regiment were then deployed in Piazza Garibaldi in front of the fascist federation, to prevent any violent events. During the following night, some military patrols controlled the streets of the city, supported by some armored cars, but it is not clear which unit they might belong to. In Fidenza, the tanks of the CCCCXXXIII Battalion Complementi Carri M, dependent on the 33rd Regiment, were used in public order tasks and corps of tankers on foot had garrisoned buildings and plants in the town.

From the point of view of personnel, the Regiment had at least 2,200 men in charge, in the city and in the province, in the following dependent departments:

- at the barracks "Principe Amedeo" , so-called "Pilotta" in Parma:
  - Command Troops at the Depot on 2 Companies.
  - Regimental Command Company, with about 150 men.
  - Battalion Specialists on 4 Companies, commanded by Major Francesco De Filippo with a force of about 600 men, gathered all the specialized personnel, such as mechanics, engineers, electricians, radio operators. It was also called the School Battalion.
  - Depot Battalion on 2 Companies, commanded by Lieutenant Colonel Guido Cornelli, had about 300 men.
  - Regimental Music Band, dependent on the Depot Battalion.
- at the barracks "Marcucci Poltri" in Santa Fiore Square in Parma:
  - II Training Battalion on 4 Companies, commanded by Major Cesare Pensato, had about 400 men, undergoing training for the passage to the P26 / 40 tanks[16].
- at the barracks "Castelletto" in Parma:
  - III Training Battalion on 4 Companies (3 of which are intended for training for self-propelled tanks and 1 for Camionette[17]). The Battalion was commanded, on Armistice Day, by Captain Elio Modesti and was equipped with 3 self-propelled guns.
  - Compagnia Mezzi Training with a staff of about 100 men, had a dozen tanks, including 2 M13 / 40 tanks and an unknown number of 47/32 L40 self-propelled vehicles, as well as some trucks and motorcycles. The vehicles were temporarily deployed to the various departments for training needs.
  - Repair and Recovery Department, with a strength of about a hundred men, had a workshop and some heavy trucks.
  - Training department, made up of veterans of the Sicilian campaign of the CCXXXIII Self-Propelled Battalion L40, arrived in Parma around mid-August and awaiting reorganization[18].
  -

16 From a report by Colonel Boldrini reported by Mario Zannoni in "Parma 1943, 8 settembre", work cited in the bibliography.

17 The Truck Company was established on 5 August, with a (theoretical) endowment of 8 machines; it is not clear whether it was the AS42 or the Desertiche model 43, nor if the cars, which were parked in the garage at the "Pilotta", were armed. It appears that the men had started training very recently when the Armistice arrived.

18 This Department should not be confused with the "Sicily" Provisional Battalion, established on July 21, 1943, following an order from General Roatta, which required to concentrate the Sicilian soldiers who, as volunteers, wished to go and set up special units to be sent against the Anglo-Americans on the island. The Battalion established in Parma was, moreover, initially placed in the employ of the 33rd Tank Regiment, a detail that increases the confusion even more.

- in Langhirano (PR):
  - I Training Battalion on 4 Companies, commanded by Major Giuseppe Stracuzzi. The 700-strong unit, almost exclusively recruits of the 1924 class, was equipped with only 2 L3 tanks, completely devoid of ammunition. In Langhirano there was also a shooting range in the bed of the Parma stream.
- in Fidenza (PR):
  - 33rd 20mm Cannon Company, commanded by Captain Gaetano Morano, with a force of 80 men, it was armed with 8 20mm machine guns, self-transporting.
  - 133rd 20mm Cannon Company, commanded by Captain Pinotto Marogna, with a force of 80 men, it was armed with 8 20mm machine guns, self-transportable. The task of both companies was to provide air protection to the tank departments of the Regiment.
  - CCCCXXXIII Battalion Complements M tanks on 4 Companies, was commanded by Major Venceslao Rossi, could have 420 men [19], all complements.

This last department, although it was the one with the best armored vehicles, among those present in the area, was in fact a training unit dependent on the 33rd Tank Regiment, which was supposed to provide men for the reconstitution of the armored units in formation, after the losses suffered in North Africa. The Battalion was located near the barracks installed in the premises of the old Rocca, it had numerous armored vehicles including M15 / 42 tanks and 75/18 M42 self-propelled tanks. concentrated in the current Foro Boario and partly along the ring road under makeshift shelters. The CCCCXXXIII Battalion Complements Carri M had become the protagonist of a particular episode on the previous 26 July. In fact, the "Emiliano" Blackshirt Battalion, coming from Dalmatia, had been in Fidenza for about a month, a department that refused to obey the order that required the Militia departments to replace the lictor beams with the stars of the Royal Army. The military authorities, consequently, ordered the CCCCXXXIII to intervene: the unit sided with its tanks around the school where the "Emiliano" Battalion had settled. The Blackshirts laid down their weapons and, aboard a train, were taken to their own depot, where the unit was demobilized.

The Command of the Armored Division "Littorio" was also present in Parma: although the large unit had been destroyed and had never been reconstituted, a small number of soldiers were still found in a building in via XXIII July. In addition to various territorial and educational departments, in the city there was also the depot of the 19th Cavalry Regiment "Guide", with 5 cavalry squadrons, but completely devoid of armored vehicles.

In Parma in the weeks preceding 8 September the German military device had grown and by 20 August already had 12,500 men, reinforced by some Panther tanks and Marder tank destroyers.

The morale of the Italian departments located in and around the city was quite weak because they were non-operational units (not only the tank crews, but all the departments present), whose supply situation was quite critical: there were numerous cases of military without uniformed, many departments were without weapons or ammunition, vehicles of any type were in short supply. The 33rd Tank Infantry Regiment was no exception. Although the departments were subjected to continuous training, fire exercises were rare and insufficient, due to the lack of ammunition, and discontent and resignation spread among the military.[20]. It was in this climate that the city found itself facing the consequences of the Armistice.

19 According to other sources, the staff was between 600 and 700 men.

20 On May 15, even, in an attempt to give a boost to the morale of the men dependent on him, Colonel Boldrini ordered to have "warrior songs" sung daily, but after three weeks it was found that the soldiers were entertaining themselves by singing tunes of a very different kind. ...

Already a few hours after the announcement made by Badoglio on the radio, Parma was filled with anxiety, when, around midnight, groups of anti-fascists went to the Command of the Military Presidium in search of information and above all weapons: the Commander of Piazza Generale Moramarco he tried to calm people by communicating that the German troops were leaving the city. In reality, starting at 8 pm, the German troops had begun their planned movements to occupy the key points of Parma, while contradictory provisions were provided to our soldiers, only partially ready in the barracks.

The German attack on the Emilian city started around 1:00 am on 9 September: after occupying the Town Hall, the German commander Lieutenant Colonel of the SS Albert Frey went to General Moramarco, ordering the surrender of the Military Presidium within 20 minutes. Moramarco, impressed by the German threat to bomb Parma (in reality a mere tactical expedient), initially accepted the surrender proposals, issuing the provisions to the dependent departments, but, having contacted the Piacenza Area Command, received an order. to resist to the bitter end. General Moramarco therefore had to revoke the provisions just issued.

The surrender order had just arrived at the "Pilotta" barracks, where the bulk of the 33rd Tank Regiment was located, when Colonel Boldrini communicated the counter-order by telephone to his subordinates: putting all departments in a state of defense and recall to the city of the units located in Langhirano and Fidenza. Boldrini communicated with his men only by telephone because, after the interview with Moramarco at the Military Presidium in Piazza ... he had inexplicably returned home. At that moment the command of the Regiment was therefore in the hands of Lieutenant Colonel Ruocco, who sent his subordinates to call the officers who were at rest in their homes back to the barracks.

The Germans in the meantime had already blocked the bridges of the city and had set up their own units in front of the barracks where the Italian soldiers were located. The first clashes took place at the Palazzo delle Poste, where a group of only nine soldiers from the 84th Territorial Battalion bis resisted the enemy attacks, until reinforcements arrived, about 25 soldiers under the command of a Lieutenant, gathered among the employees of the Battalion barracks services. In reinforcement of the small defense squad at the TIMO telephone exchange, the 33rd Carristi had, in the meantime, sent a platoon of 50 men on foot, under the command of Lieutenant Menoni and Lieutenant Ruggeri. Meanwhile, the Command of the Military Presidium, hit by an artillery attack, surrendered almost immediately and the other barracks were also in serious difficulty, both for the better armament of the German units, and for the delay with which the local commands had taken countermeasures for the defense of the city. At 3:00 the Germans launched an attack on the Infantry and Tank Application School, which was located in the Doge's Palace, which surrendered four hours later.

The "Castelletto" barracks, where part of the 33rd Tank is located, was surrounded at around 4:00 by soldiers of the 1st Company of the 1st Battalion of the 1st Armored Regiment of the SS: the Germans had intended to overwhelm the barracks quickly, since they knew that some armored vehicles were inside. Captain Modesti, who commanded the departments headquartered in the "Castelletto", after receiving an order by telephone from Boldrini to prepare for the defense, sending tanks and motorcyclists to reconnaissance in the surroundings, lost precious moments in the indecision on what to do, and so the garrison it had to suffer the sudden German attack. Captain Modesti immediately communicated to the Regimental Command that he was under attack, receiving orders to resist, awaiting reinforcements recalled from out of town. The situation, however, was severely compromised and Captain Modesti accepted the surrender offered by the Germans.

At the same time, the "Pilotta" barracks were also stormed by the Germanic units. Around 3:00 am, while most of the officers had returned to the barracks, Colonel Boldrini was cut off, because the bridges over the Parma stream were now manned by the Germans, and consequently the Adjutant Major Lieutenant Colonel Ruocco assumed command of the Regiment and its dependent departments and Lieutenant Colonel Musa that of the barracks, while Boldrini began to give orders by telephone. The only force that would have been able to offer serious resistance was the tanks and self-propelled vehicles of the CCCCXXXIII Battalion of Major Rossi and the 1st Training Battalion of Langhirano. At 3.30 from the "Pilotta" barracks, Lieutenant Colonel Ruocco contacted Major Rossi, giving him instructions to converge on Parma with as many armored vehicles and machine gunners as possible, justifying the order with vague reasons of public order, and instructing him to bring his departments at the Caprazucca bridge, where he would have been joined by Colonel Boldrini, who would have provided further details[21]. Since telephone communications with Langhirano were interrupted, Ruocco was ordered to send a relay to the 1st Training Battalion, but the runner could not even leave the "Pilotta", since the barracks were already surrounded by the Germans.[22]. In the meantime, inside the "Pilotta" barracks, the distribution of the few weapons and ammunition available began, and while a defensive belt was prepared, supported by only three machine guns available, Lieutenant Colonel Musa gave the order to prepare the vans parked in the shed, to attempt a sortie pending the arrival of reinforcements from Fidenza, as per telephone orders from Colonel Boldrini. In the meantime, in fact, a platoon of the 1st Company of the 1st SS Battalion, supported by a pair of self-propelled anti-aircraft, had tightened around the barracks, then managed to force the entrance, while the squad of Lieutenant Menoni tried to return to the barracks. At the moment when the officers ordered the tankmen to cease all unnecessary resistance, a group of German soldiers broke into the office of Lieutenant Colonel Ruocco, just as Captain Orlando was trying, in vain, to secure the flag of the Regiment. At 5.30 in the barracks of the "Pilotta" any attempt to resist had been stifled. The main military structures of the city were now in German hands and the Italian soldiers taken prisoner were concentrated in the Citadel: the last hopes of the Italian Command lay in the reinforcements arriving from Langhirano. Meanwhile, Lieutenant Colonel Frey gave orders to create barrages, supported by artillery, on the main access roads of the city, fearing the arrival of the Italian units located in the province.

In Langhirano, meanwhile, Major Venceslao Rossi, despite not having clear the meaning of the order received from Parma, had organized the rescue column, many Tankers had volunteered, but, given the limited number of vehicles available, not all they could take part in the action. Around 5:30 in the morning, the column was set in motion, made up of a training tank company, with a strength of about one hundred soldiers (especially from the 3rd Company), 1 wagon M15 / 42 and

21 However, the reasons for this apparently senseless order are not known, given that the Germans had practically occupied all the key points in the city. Some argue that the action should have had as its objective the breaking of the Germanic encirclement, but it is not clear why, at that time, the order was given to have only a small part of the personnel and not the entire Battalion leave from Fidenza. Another interpretation maintains that the Piazza di Parma Command called the department back to the city to carry out a public order service, an order which, however, would not explain the dispatch of the self-propelled vehicles. On the other hand, not even the official military sources allow to clarify the question exactly. In fact, the commander of the 33rd Tank Regiment, on which the CCCCXXXIII Battalion depended, gave only a brief report: *"On September 8, 1943, the command of the Regiment issued orders for armed resistance to the Germans and for a counterattack hinged on the convergence of two columns, coming from Fidenza and Langhirano, on Parma. The execution of these orders had only partial possibility of realization. The column of self-propelled and anti-aircraft coming from Fidenza sustained for a few hours, on the morning of 9 September, near the Parma stream, a fight against German armored units, resulting in significant losses in dead, wounded and prisoners".*

22 It is also probable that the Germans, in some way, had kept the movements of the Italian tanks under control and that consequently they were aware of the departure in the night between 8 and 9 September towards Parma, being prepared with a line of well-conceived anti-tank defense. Among other things, Colonel Boldrini had ordered to send a non-commissioned officer to meet the column, to give more precise provisions. The Sergeant who had received this order, aboard a FIAT 508CM, was however captured by the Germans as he was leaving Parma and, probably, forced to provide information on his mission.

7 self-propelled 75/18 M42[23], and a training cannon company with about fifty soldiers, 12 SPA Dovunque trucks, carrying as many 20 mm machine guns, 2 Bianchi Miles trucks, one of which was destined for the transport of anti-aircraft gun ammunition, and 2 Guzzi motorcycles. The Tank Training Company was commanded by Lieutenant Giuseppe Riservato (the tanks had a very limited supply of ammunition on board, as if they had to participate in an exercise, only 5 grenades each), while the rate of the armed trucks was commanded by the Captain Pinotto Marogna. On board the two motorcycles, the Private Lieutenant opened the column, while the adjutant Major Lieutenant Cornini kept the connections between the head and the tail. Germanic relays soon intercepted the column shortly after Pontetaro, managing to count the Italian vehicles in motion, and the Germans thus prepared to ambush the entrance to the city, after having prepared defensive barriers. The "visit" of the German motorcyclists did not bode well and the order was therefore given to dispose of the bullets of the armored vehicles. Around 6 o'clock the column reached Parma and, after crossing Barriera d'Azeglio and taking Viale dei Mille, a snake of German trucks deliberately cut off the road to the Italian tanks, preventing them from continuing for several minutes, as long as the Italian tankers they noticed that the trucks that made up the carousel were always the same, that, turning repeatedly around the block, seemed to form an infinite column. However, this maneuver had allowed, at the same time, the placing in battery of two positions of German anti-tank guns, one of which at the entrance to Ponte Italia (then Ponte Umberto), and a machine gun nest. Resuming the march to Barriera Bixio, headed for viale Caprera, in training training, the tanks came into contact with the German positions, after the two Italian tank officers on motorcycles had identified the opposing positions. Unfortunately, the Lieutenant Reserved, having passed the column to continue his patrol towards Ponte Umberto, was captured by the Germans; at the same time in piazzale Marsala, the Germans opened fire on the Italian column and the shots of the German guns immediately hit the fourth self-propelled machine in the center of the formation, which caught fire. Sergeant Jovino, who threw himself out of the tank with his suit on fire, was immediately mowed down by a barrage of machine guns, while Tanker Strapponi managed to get out surrounded by flames, dying burnt alongside the tank[24]. The only one to save himself was the commander Grassi, who, after being wounded by the armored vehicle, collapsed not far away, being rescued by some civilians. A second self-propelled[25] managed to overwhelm the German position, pushing the cannon into an escarpment, but at the same time the self-propelled machine of Lieutenant Valente was hit in the right track, the pilot Caporalmaggiore Giavazzoli lost control and the vehicle crashed into the Parma stream[26]. Giavazzoli died instantly, Caporalmaggiore Ledro, a radio operator, was probably injured in agony for hours under the Umberto bridge, invoking help, while Valente, recovering from fainting, managed to take shelter in a hole, where he waited for darkness to fall.

The other three self-propelled, that of Lieutenant Semprini[27], that of Lieutenant Bagnoli and that of Sergeant Major Cavirani, managed to force the blockade and enter the city, crossing the Umberto bridge unscathed, but were blocked one after the other by the shots of anti-tank pieces: the first stopped at via Passo Buole, the second at via Vitali and the third just before Barriera Farini. Bagnoli then took via Passo Buole, to escape the fire of the anti-tank pieces brought in all haste by the Germans, but was hit by an armor-piercing bullet: the crew, exiting the vehicle, were quickly captured by the Germans, but only an instant after the Lieutenant Bagnoli had sabotaged the gun, throwing

23 According to a source, there were 8 self-propelled guns.

24 His body had been made unrecognizable by the flames, so much so that only after many years it was possible to attribute his identity.

25 It is not clear if it was the vehicle of Lieutenant Semprini (the first of the column) or that of the Second Lieutenant Valente (the third of the column).

26 According to other sources, Lieutenant Valente's self-propelled vehicle still managed to ram a German tank, dragging it with it into the water.

27 Other sources report that Semprini commanded the column's M15 / 42 wagon.

the bolt into a nearby garden. The self-propelled machine belonging to Lieutenant Semprini was instead miraculously captured intact by the Germans. The only vehicle still in motion, that of Sergeant Major Cavirani, after heading towards the Citadel, ended up under enemy fire and, if a first anti-tank bullet missed it, going to hit a house, the second instead made it fatally havoc in the back. All the crews, captured by the Germans, were thus led to the Citadel, where there were already other Italian prisoners. The vehicle of Lieutenant Semprini was also brought here and the three capicars Semprini, Cavirani and Bagnoli, for a moment, toyed with the idea of getting on board the Semprini vehicle, left unattended, to try to free the Italian prisoners.

Intent, the three self-propelled vehicles under the command of Major Rossi, who remained at the entrance to Parma, in Barriera Bixio, with their trucks and machine gunners, engaged in a fire fight with the Germanic troops. The 20 mm guns were unloaded from the trucks and placed in battery around the barrier gates, because in the meantime the Germans had recovered the anti-tank gun from the embankment where it had been thrown. The three self-propelled vehicles were located in order to keep viale Caprera, via Solari and via Spezia under control. While Lieutenant Cornini, sent in command of the "Pilotta", was wounded by the Germans, Major Rossi was reached by a written message from Colonel Boldrini, who ordered him to resist and try to occupy the Dattaro bridge, from where they should have arrived. the expected reinforcements from Langhirano. During the battle two self-propelled machines were put out of use (the one in viale Caprera and the one next to Barriera Bixio, in defense of via Solari) and the human losses were huge, while the gunners, exposed to enemy fire, because the machine gunners were not shielded. there were no shelters of any kind, they continued firing uninterruptedly. A student officer, Lieutenant Francesco Villari, unable to reach the Application School, presented himself to the unit at Barriera Bixio, where he asked to be able to lend a hand to the defense, but was killed during the clash. At 7:30 the truck carrying the ammunition of the 20 mm machine guns exploded and at 8:00, when the ammunition ran out, the valiant Italian soldiers had to surrender, not without having sabotaged the vehicles. The Germans began to rake the area, in order to capture all the Italian soldiers who were trying to get away, and recovered the surviving self-propelled machine and the 20 mm machine guns[28]. The battle was short, but uneven and bloody, so much so that the echo of the explosions reached Fontanellato, as told in his diary by a British prisoner interned there: "*9 September - I woke up that morning, just when it was starting to dawn, about 6. As I lay awake thinking about getting out of bed, I realized there were many explosions in the distance. Later we learned that there was a battle between Germans and Italians for the Parma railway station*". The tankers and gunners of this unfortunate column paid another toll in this latest attempt at resistance. In fact, the Second Lieutenants Antonio Manazza of the Cannoni Company and Francesco Villari lost their lives[29], Sergeant Major Franco Jovino, Corporal Francesco Giavazzoli and the Carristi Achille Piacentini and Giuseppe Strepponi, all very young. For a few days the tanks of the CCCCXXXIII Battalion, damaged by enemy fire, were left in the streets before being removed.

The "Marcucci Poltri" barracks, where the II Training Battalion was based, was completely ignored by the Germans, and, during the morning at the end of the fighting, Colonel Boldrini gave permission by telephone to Major Pensato to abandon the building, to avoid to the Tankers the capture.

While the battle between the tank crews of the CCCCXXXIII Battalion Complementi Carri M and the German troops was ending in Parma, the soldiers who remained in the barracks in Fidenza became aware of the situation in the city. Among the tank crews, 300 men under the command of

28 Some of these had been deliberately put out of use by the servants, when the fate of the battle was now sealed.
29 Lieutenant Villari, as we have seen, was a student officer of the Application School who, unable to reach the headquarters, had joined the column of tankers.

Captain Traversa, restlessness began to spread, exacerbated by the lack of orders and the arrival of an SS unit in the town started a general stampede. The Germans managed to gather about 200 stray tankers in the train station, but here, with the help of some employees of the Royal Railways, the Italian soldiers managed to escape to safety on the sly.

In Langhirano, meanwhile, the 1st Training Battalion had been cut off from communications, but, around 7:30, news of what was happening in Parma arrived. There was a council between the commanders of the 4 Companies and Major Stracuzzi, at the end of which they prepared to resist a possible attack, despite the fact that the commanders of the Companies had proposed to bring the Battalion to the surrounding hills. On his own initiative, Captain Giuseppe Febbo, commander of the 2nd Company, had all the ammunition available in the warehouse delivered and distributed them among his men. In the early afternoon the first German soldiers arrived and surprised the 3rd and 4th Company, located in a factory, alarming the rest of the Battalion. Captain Febbo immediately crossed the Parma stream with his men, making the Company camp out in anticipation of the events. Major Stracuzzi, with the 1st Company commanded by Captain Bai-Macario, went into a wood to escape capture; here he disbanded the unit, ordering to bury the weapons. Only the 2nd Company of the 1st Training Battalion remained in arms for several days. The unit, as we have seen, camped on the hills southeast of Langhirano, supported by the help of the local population, who supplied the soldiers with food. Wearing civilian clothes, Febbo and some of his officers tried to reunite with some Italian command in the area, but, faced with the total collapse they witnessed, the Captain gathered his 180 men on September 20, ordered to hide the weapons, and gave disposition his men to go away in small groups, to try to return to their families and, if possible, to cross the enemy lines to reach the South and the royal forces that were beginning to reorganize. Captain Febbo managed to reach Lanciano (CH), where on 3 December he presented himself to the authorities of the Royal Army, who were traveling up the Peninsula with the Allies.

Colonel Boldrini, commander of the 33rd Tank Infantry Regiment, attempted to reach Langhirano in the afternoon of 9 September by bicycle, accompanied by two other officers, but, having received news of what happened to the 1st Training Battalion, aware that there was nothing more to to do, he saved himself by taking refuge with acquaintances.

3. Piacenza

On the morning of September 9, two tanks of the 33rd Tank Regiment arrived from Fidenza to Piacenza, after the local Military Presidium had sent a request for help[30]: the city had in fact been hit by a ferocious attack by Germanic armored units. The two tanks immediately took part in the clashes but were quickly hit and put out of use and four tankers died at that juncture: the first tank was hit at 10 am and was immobilized and Corporal Roberto Sampaolo died there. The second tank tried to rescue the first but was hit by the bombs of the enemy aviation stationed in San Damiano: the pilot Franco Dall'Aquila died instantly, while the Second Lieutenant Gugliemo Dimeo could not be rescued. No better fate had a third tank, probably one of those posted in the town on July 26, and the crew had a bad end: Sergeant Lorenzo Corratella died instantly, the seriously injured Tank driver Capelli was saved but suffered, two months, after the amputation of the legs.

30 As early as July 26, officially for reasons of public order, two tanks of the CCCCXXIII Complementi Battalion stationed in Fidenza, had been deployed in Piacenza under the command of Lieutenant Ugo Fracassi.

4. Sardinia

Although it had gradually lost strategic importance, after the loss of Sicily, at the time of the Armistice Sardinia was garrisoned by 4 Mobile Divisions and 3 Coastal Divisions, organized into two Corps, which totaled 5,108 officers and 126,946 between non-commissioned officers and men of troop. On 8 September, the "Scalabrino" Motorized Armored Group was also present in Sardinia, established in March 1943, consisting of:

- 32nd Tank Regiment, commanded by General Ercole Calvi, consisting of:
    - Command (located in Sanluri)
    - Command Platoon (located in Sanluri)
    - Regimental Workshop (located in Monti)
    - II L35 Tank Battalion, located in Sanluri; commanded by Lieutenant Colonel Luigi Longo, it was placed under the command of the "Nembo" Parachute Division and a Company of the Battalion was located in Tempio Pausania.
    - XVI M41 Tank Battalion, located in Ozieri under the command of Major Furla
    - CC Somua Tank Battalion, located in Dolianova, was commanded by Captain Dal Pozzo and depended on the 13th Army Corps for use[31]
    - 9th Motor Gun Company
    - 10th Motor Gun Company
    - 11th Motor Gun Company
    - 13th Motor Gun Company
    - 2nd Company of the I Anti-Tank Battalion from 47/32DLXI 75/18 Self-propelled Group
- 195th Legion M.V.S.N.
- I Artillery Group from 75/27
- I Artillery Group from 100/17
- XXI Autonomous Infantry Battalion.

The DLXI 75/18 Self-Propelled Group had been established at the depot of the 131st Artillery Regiment of Livorno in the second half of 1942, becoming dependent on the "Friuli" Infantry Division in May of the following year and reaching full staff only in the month of august. The department was equipped with 18 self-propelled 75/18 trucks and 2 command wagons, as well as 35 old FIAT

31 Germany had sold 32 (or 33, according to sources) Somua S35 wagons to Italy, against a request of 50, to organize an "Experimental Mixed Company", to be used in North Africa, consisting of:

- Armored car platoon
- R35 tank platoon
- S35 tank platoon.

Only the armored car platoon was actually sent to Africa, the S35 tanks were instead sent, without spare parts, to Sardinia, going to equip the CC Battalion of the 131st Tank Regiment from June 1941, which after basic training was transferred to the Veneto in the following July. With a circular dated December 15, 1941, the Battalion, out of only two Companies, was transferred to Sardinia and was incorporated into the 32nd Tank Regiment on September 20, 1942. Commanded by Major Enzo del Pozzo, it became part of the "Scalabrino" Motorboat Group in March 1943. At the time of the Armistice, the Somua tanks were not in optimal condition and did not participate in major operations during the military events that followed 8 September on the island.

18BL trucks and 23 SPA CL39 trucks. The Group (minus 1 Battery) formed the "Ravot" Motorcycle Armored Group, together with the 1st M Tank Company. The other Battery of the Group and the CC Somua Tank Battalion were employed by the 13th Army Corps. On the island there was also the XVIII M Tank Battalion, which depended on the Command of the XXX Corps.

The Group, which had taken its name from its commander, Brigadier General Giovanni Maria Scalabrino, was based in San Gavino (SU) and formally depended on the XIII Corps, with functions of cover and anti-landing troops, with a staff of 180 officers, 319 non-commissioned officers and 2,578 troops. The unit had been divided into two tactical groups, one of which was located between Tempio Pausania (SS) and Olbia, the so-called "Monti Logistics Area", where food, ammunition and fuel were stored in anticipation of an allied landing.

The units of the Motorized Armored Group reacted decisively to the proclamation of the Armistice, thwarting the German attempt to take over the Group's Command on the morning of 9 September, putting pressure on the German troops stationed on the island, so that they were pushed from the inside. towards the coastal strip, to prevent them heading north, to the embarkation ports. On 15 September the XVI M Tank Battalion, supported by a company of motor gunners and 2 infantry, occupied the German depots in Monti, and the following day the Italian troops were divided into two columns, the "Di Nisio" column, reinforced by a company of self-propelled vehicles, and the "Garelli" Column, to which the XVI Medium Tank Battalion was attached. The rest of the "Scalabrino" Grouping had moved between Teti and Scalangius, with the support of 18 Somua tanks of the CC Battalion and 6 self-propelled tanks of the DLXI Self-propelled Group of 75/18, urging the Germans, who were moving north island: unfortunately many of the Somua S35 were in bad conditions and could only make a limited contribution to the operations. On the 17th the units of the "Nembo" Division, supported by the 2nd L35 Tank Battalion, began operations to free the Campidano and Sarcidano area. On 18 September, the German troops, to escape the fighting with the Italians, began to embark to leave the island, ending operations on 20. On 2 October there were the last fallen of the Group, the Sergeant Major Lodovico Marafon and the Corporal Edoardo Galletti, who died aboard their two 47/32 self-propelled machines, which exploded on a mine during the occupation of a built-up area.

The departments of the "Scalabrino" group remained in garrison on the island until August 1944, amidst mixed fortunes (the 32nd Regiment was dissolved on October 2), as we will see in the next chapter.

5. Other episodes of resistance

On 8 September the 2nd "Emanuele Filiberto Testa di Ferro" Celere Division was returning from France, which included the "San Marco" Group II and the "Piemonte Reale" III Group. The "San Marco" was disarmed on the way back to Italy, while the "Piemonte Reale" reached the Turin belt without problems. Between Nichelino, Caraglio, Villafalletto and Savigliano the I Squadron L6 Tanks of the "Piemonte Reale" opposed the German troops in several firefights. On 12th September, in compliance with the orders received and after having saved the banner, the Group was disarmed along with the rest of the Division. The 3rd L Tanks Group "San Giorgio", which was being reconstituted in Piedmont, was instead entirely captured.

At the end of August a L40 self-propelled Platoon of the IV Armored Group "Alessandria" had been sent to Val Canale from Codroipo (UD), after German units had entered Italy from the Tarvisio pass. At the time of the Armistice, this unit reacted to the Germanic movements, unfortunately without having any success.

▲ M15 / 42 tanks of the 19th Battalion of the 31st Tank Regiment during the clashes of 11 September 1943 in Piombino. The vehicles, which appear camouflaged in three tones according to the standard of the period, should be located near the "Pacinotti" Technical Institute, in the distance you can see the bell tower of the church of Sant'Antimo (private collection via Niccolò Tognarini).

▼ Some soldiers of the Kriegsmarine and, probably, of the Luftwaffe, pose in front of one of the M15 / 42s of the 19th Battalion, captured at the end of the 11 September clashes. The image allows you to appreciate the camouflage of the vehicles, on which you can still see the plate of the Royal Army (private collection via Niccolò Tognarini).

▲ After the battle of Piombino, the tanks of the 19th Battalion of the 31st Tank Regiment were probably piled up in some locality of the city, waiting to be destined for some German armored unit, as evidenced by these photographs taken on 10 November 1943 (private collection via Niccolò Tognarini).

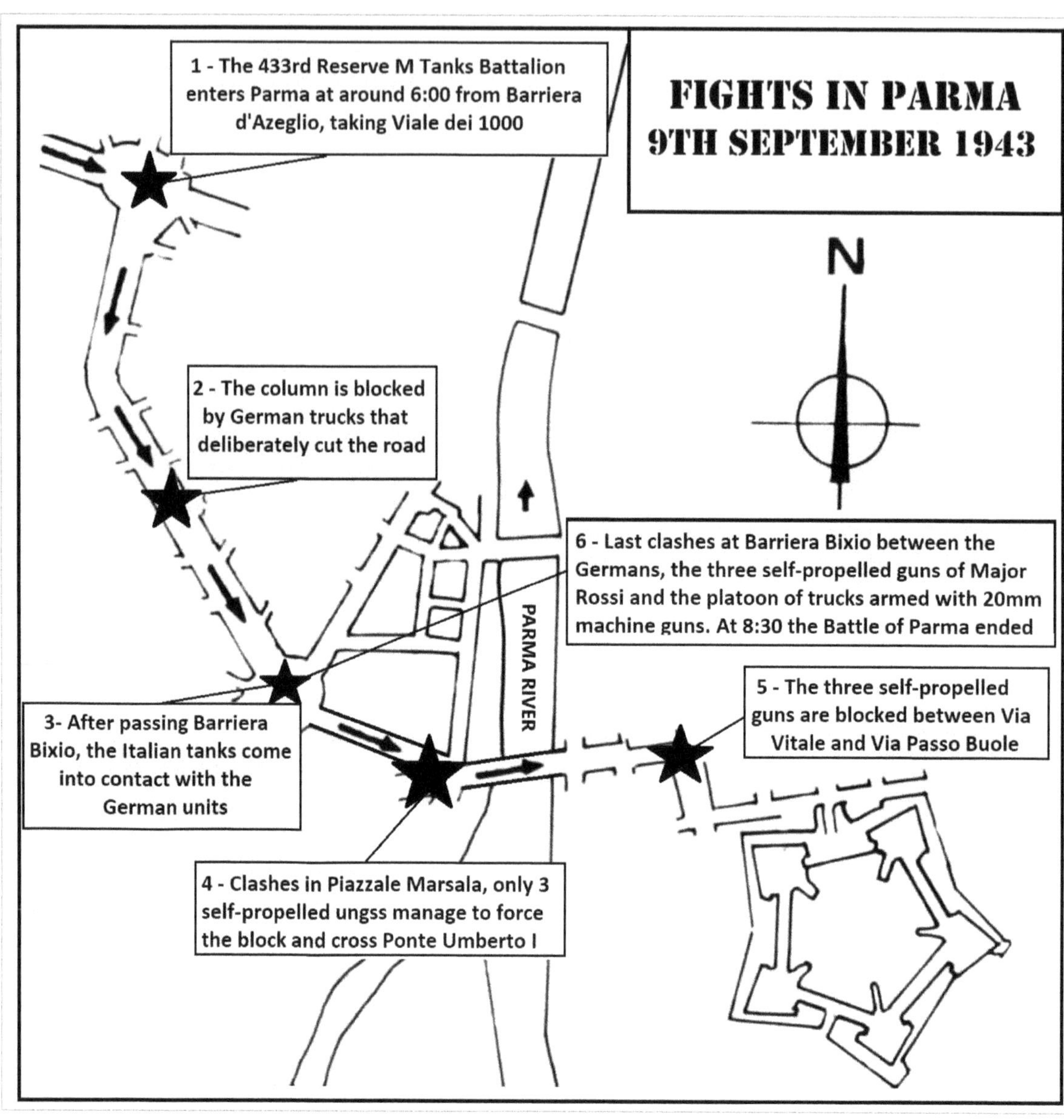
FIGHTS IN PARMA
9TH SEPTEMBER 1943
N
1 - The 433rd Reserve M Tanks Battalion enters Parma at around 6:00 from Barriera d'Azeglio, taking Viale dei 1000
2 - The column is blocked by German trucks that deliberately cut the road
3- After passing Barriera Bixio, the Italian tanks come into contact with the German units
4 - Clashes in Piazzale Marsala, only 3 self-propelled ungss manage to force the block and cross Ponte Umberto I
5 - The three self-propelled guns are blocked between Via Vitale and Via Passo Buole
6 - Last clashes at Barriera Bixio between the Germans, the three self-propelled guns of Major Rossi and the platoon of trucks armed with 20mm machine guns. At 8:30 the Battle of Parma ended
PARMA RIVER

▲ Two M13 / 40 tanks of the 33rd Tank Regiment garrison Piazza Garibaldi in Parma, near the local fascist federation, on July 26, 1943 (Manes).

▼ Boys and children around an Italian 75/18 M42 self-propelled vehicle belonging to the CCCXXXIII Battalion Complementi Carri M struck in piazzale Marsala in Parma (Manes).

▲ The headquarters of the Parma military garrison at the end of the clashes in which the Italian units tried to protect the city from German occupation. The shots fired by the German canons during the battle (Manes) are evident on the facade of the building.

▲ The self-propelled 75/18 car belonging to Lieutenant Valente, which fell into the bed of the Parma stream after being hit by a track (Manes).

▲ One of the self-propelled vehicles of the CCCXXXIII Complementi Battalion immobilized at Barriera Bixio during the clashes of 9 September 1943 (Manes).

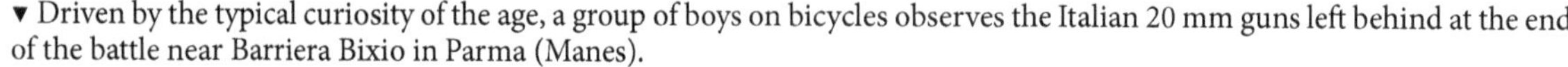

▼ Driven by the typical curiosity of the age, a group of boys on bicycles observes the Italian 20 mm guns left behind at the end of the battle near Barriera Bixio in Parma (Manes).

▲ In this image the self-propelled vehicle that had been placed in defense of viale Caprera: the vehicle appears severely damaged (Manes).

▼ These French Somua S35 war prey wagons are waiting to be shipped to Sardinia, assigned to the CC Battalion of the 131st Tank Regiment. The vehicles are painted in dark green color and bear a curious symbol on the turret, depicting the profile of a rhinoceros, in white or blue (A.S.S.Fort Sardegna via Giovanni Olla).

▲ Another of the self-propelled vehicles that fought in Parma at Barriera Bixio, next to the Dazio building, near Viale dei Mille. Note the hole in one of the anti-tank shells, which hit the tank right next to the "RE 6457" (Manes) plate.

▲ Officers of the 33rd Tank Infantry Regiment in conversation with SS officer after the surrender of the troops of Parma (Manes).

▲ Commemorative plaque for the tankers who died on 9 September 1943, placed in piazzale Marsala in Parma, in the place that was the fulcrum of the fight.

▲ In the photo, on the right indicated by the arrow, Corporal Roberto Sampaolo of the 33rd Tank Infantry Regiment, who died in Piacenza in his tank while fighting the German troops (Carlini).

▲ An L3 / 33 Flamethrower stationed in an olive grove in Sardinia (D'Alessandro).

▼ L3 / 35 tank of the Del Brocco tanker in Sardinia: the vehicle is almost completely covered by dust, which creates a sort of natural camouflage (Del Brocco).

THE REACTION OF THE ARMORED UNITS ABROAD

Even for the armored units that were outside the national borders, the evening of 8 September opened a particularly difficult moment of transition, creating an absolute confusion, made more acute by the distance from the motherland. The resistance of the Italian military abroad is a fairly unknown chapter of those terrible moments, in fact the facts of Leros and Kefalonia are known, because they are often mentioned on the occasion of the anniversary of "April 25", but the many others are less known. episodes in which Italian military units resisted the Germans to the limit of their operational capacity. It is true that the royal armed forces reacted in an uncoordinated manner to the news of the Armistice, many units disbanded, trying to return to Italy, and only small units continued to fight alongside the German ally, but there were also more or less consistent reactions. by armored units (and not only), which did not give up their arms and turned against the Germans, especially in Corsica, where the resistance was fierce and organic.

On Armistice Day, these armored units were located outside the national borders:

- in France:
  - L6/40 Tank Squadron Group (in Southern France)
  - 3 L Tank Battalions, 2 47/32 Self-Propelled Battalions and other minor units in Corsica (we will see the details in the next paragraph)
- in Albania:
  - DLXVIII 75/18 Self-propelled Group
  - CXXXII 47/32 Self-Propelled Battalion
- In Jugoslavia:
  - Autonomous Company Carri (Zara)
  - Autonomous Company Armored Car (Ljubljana)[32]
  - 1st Battalion of the 31st Tank Infantry Regiment (Croatia)
  - III Battalion of the 31st Tank Infantry Regiment (Montenegro)
  - 1st L Tank Group "San Giusto" (between Kvarner and Dalmatia)
  - 2nd L Tank Group "San Marco" (Dubrovnik and Spalato)
  - numerous platoons and autonomous companies of tanks and armored cars
- in the Dodecanese:
  - CCCXII Mixed Tank Battalion (Rhodes)
  - 51st Autonomous L3 Tank Company (Crete)

Now let's see in detail the events that these units went through.

32 Originated by the "Nizza Cavalry" Regiment.

6. Corsica

Corsica had been occupied by the Italians in November 1942 and at the time of the Armistice the VII Corps, commanded by General Magli, which had about 60,900 soldiers, was garrisoned. The Italian Command in Corsica was located at the Hotel "de la Paix" in Corte, a town with a fortified citadel in the central-northern mountains of the island.

That in Corsica was the only victorious resistance in French territory; the following armored units were present on the island:

- CXXXI 47/32 Self-Propelled Battalion of the "Cremona" Infantry Division. It came from the depot of the 31st Tank Regiment of Siena and was assigned to the "Cremona", sent to Corsica in November 1942 following the allied landing in Algeria and Tunisia.
- XX 47/32 Self-Propelled Battalion, commanded by Lieutenant Colonel Alessandro Minelli, assigned to the "Friuli" Division. The Battalion was formed at the Verona Depot of the 32nd Tank Regiment.
- XIII L Tank Battalion, coming from the 33rd Tank Regiment, under the command of Major Antonio Anedda, was mostly equipped with modernized L3 / 38 light tanks. The Battalion, stationed in Sardinia, was sent to Corsica during the occupation of the island in November 1942. It had a staff of 22 officers, 32 non-commissioned officers and 316 troops and was divided into:
    - Command Company
    - 1st Tank Company
    - 2nd Tank Company
    - Motor Gun Company
- 1st L Tank Battalion of the 33rd Tank Regiment, commanded by Major Gaspare Calcara, on:
    - Command Company (with 2 L3/35 tanks e 2 L6/40 tanks)
    - 1st Company (with 13 L3/35 tanks)
    - 2nd Company (with 13 L3/35 tanks)
    - 3rd Company (with 13 L3/35 tanks)
- II L Tank Battalion of the 33rd Tank Regiment
- 10th Celere Group, under the command of Lieutenant Colonel Ettore Fucci. It had been set up with Battalions and Companies detached from Deposits and Regiments, to be made available to the VII Corps in Corsica. The Group was constituted at the Court, where the Italian Command was located; composed of Alpini and Bersaglieri, it was a sort of rapid intervention force, to be used for any eventuality in every part of the island. It was formed by:
    - Command
    - XXXIII Battalion Bersaglieri Cyclists[33]
    - LXXI Motorized Bersaglieri Battalion
    - 107th Motorcyclists Company
    - 7th Armored Car Company, on Command Platoon and 4 Armored Car Platoons, with 17 AB41 armored cars[34]

33 It was located in Vizzavona, a tiny town about 40 kilometers south of Corte, 900 meters high.

34 This was none other than the 1st Company of the 18th Bersaglieri Regiment, which had been detached from the original department and sent to the Lane as a reinforcement for the 10th Raggruppamento Celere.

A total of 55 47/32 L40 self-propelled vehicles, 69 L3 / 35 and L3 / 38 light tanks and 17 AB41 armored cars were available on the island.

In the second half of 1943 the Italian commands had to manage a feeling of growing hostility on the part of the French. The proportion between the Italian contingent and the inhabitants of the island was almost exaggerated, with a ratio of about one soldier for every three inhabitants, a situation that was experienced by the Corsicans as a sort of continuous provocation. The Italian authorities tried in every way to give the military presence a purely defensive character against possible Allied attacks, but the Corsicans, with the passage of time, increasingly perceived it as a real occupation.

The Italian units, who remained in the dark about the Armistice, were guarding long stretches of coast on 8 September to avoid Allied landings, while the Germans of the SS-Sturmbrigade "Reichsführer SS" were stationed in the Sartene area. In support of the latter, in the night between 8 and 9 September the 90 Panzergrenadier-Division landed in Bonifacio and immediately the Italian departments were hired by the now former allies, with lightning-fast actions that aimed at complete occupation of the island. The surprise dictated by the German attack greatly disoriented the Italian units, initially convinced that they were being attacked by American troops, but, once the situation clarified, the Italian reaction proved decisive and inflicted heavy losses on the Germans.

The port of Bastia was immediately occupied, but the units of the Royal Army managed to regain possession of it in a short time. The occupation of the port would have represented a great advantage for the Germans: on the one hand it would have precluded the Italian troops from returning to Sardinia, on the other hand they would have ensured safe access to receive reinforcements and supplies. The self-propelled units of the XX 47/32 Self-Propelled Battalion of the "Friuli" Division, which was stationed in the city, took part in the clashes.

Almost simultaneously, numerous violent clashes broke out in many parts of the island, with mixed fortunes and the port of Bastia was once again lost.

On 14 September the 4th Franco-Moroccan Division of the 1st Army Corps began to flow into the port of Ajaccio, in support of the Italian troops, and on the 23rd from Sardinia the 1st Battery of the DLXI Gruppo Semoventi from 75/18 arrived in Ajaccio, on 6 pieces; the Battery was then moved to the Court, participating in subsequent operations against the Germans, reaching as far as Bastia. From that moment, the operations on the Bastia front continued jointly and the collaboration between Italians and French to the complete defeat of the German troops between 29 September and 4 October. That day the vital port of Bastia was again recaptured, from where the Germanic armed forces were embarking to save themselves on the continent, and the next day the last German prisoners were captured.

The immediate reaction and the compactness with which the Italian units reacted to the German offensive meant that the island did not witness the terrible rout that instead took place in the Balkans, despite the fighting had been supported by the Italian units in a state of evident inferiority of armament. However, the profuse commitment allowed the undisturbed landing of the French troops and the combativeness of the Italian soldiers inflicted significant losses among the Germans, causing them a considerable delay in leaving the island.

After having eliminated the German threat in the two islands, however, the Allied commands no longer considered the presence of Italian armored units appropriate, so much so that materials, such as the radio stations of the tanks, were confiscated from the departments present in Sardinia, in order to make them unusable. , while those located in Corsica had to surrender their armored vehicles to the French degaullists. In fact, all the self-propelled vehicles from the CLXXXI and the XX Battalion were confiscated by the French departments and the two units were transferred to Sardinia (the XX Battalion on October 20 and the CLXXXI the following day), to then be transferred to the Peninsula at the end of the year. , being transformed into simple framework Battalions. On 22 October, the 1st Battery of the DLXI Gruppo Semoventi from 75/18, returned to its department in Sardinia[35], while on 17 October the XIII L Tank Battalion had landed in Palau, where it was dissolved the following month, with the exception of the Motomitraglieri Company, which remained autonomous.

The toll of Italian blood in the clashes in Corsica was high, over 600 fallen, who now rest in the cemetery of the "Wolves of Tuscany" in Livorno. During the operations in Corsica the Captain Giovanni Carta, the Second Lieutenant Giuseppe Giuliano, the Sergeant Ettore Moretti (in memory) and the Tankers Bernardino Cenni and Pietro Zanni of the CXXXI Self-Propelled Battalion from 47/32 were decorated with a Bronze Medal for Military Valor, while the Lieutenant Domenico Chicco, medical officer of the battalion, deserved a War Cross for Military Valor.

Even today, almost 80 years after the end of the Second World War, in Corsica it is easy to come across remnants of the conflict, especially cars and armored vehicles, some of which, especially in recent years, have been the subject of projects of recovery and museumization.

7. Albania

The largest unit equipped with armored vehicles in Albania was the 11th "Brenner" Division, whose 9th "Brenner" Artillery Regiment could count on the DLVIII Self-propelled Group of 75/18 M41 and the CXXXII Self-propelled Battalion Counter-tank of 47/32 , in addition to the XLVII Contraereo Group of 75/46, two Artillery Groups of 75/32 and a Group of 75/27. Overwhelmed by the tragic events of 8 September, the Division did not in fact oppose any resistance to the Germanic armed forces, breaking up in a bloodless manner and delivering weapons and equipment to the now former allies.

In Tirana, there was the IV Armored Group of the "Nice Cavalry" Regiment, under the command of Lieutenant Colonel Luigi Goytre. The unit, which depended on the 9th Army, was made up of a Squadron of 15 L6 / 40 tanks and a Squadron of 21 AB41 armored cars and carried out patrol and escort services. After the declaration of the Armistice, Lieutenant Colonel Goytre was among the first officers to vigorously oppose the Germanic armed forces and the IV Armored Group clashed severely with German units for a few days, in particular to prevent the occupation of the city's airport. Precisely during these fights, Lieutenant Colonel Goytre, who had been seriously wounded in the chest, lost his life on 12 September. For his sacrifice, on September 23, 1945 the Gold Medal for Military Valor was awarded to his memory with this motivation: "*In a tragic moment for the homeland and loss of his armed forces, keeping faith with the oath taken, he proudly opposed spirit, worthy of the noble traditions of the Italian Army, a categorical refusal to the order given to him to surrender his arms to the Germans and to surrender. Even though he was aware of the serious risks he was voting on he reacted immediately by organizing an honorable reaction. Having failed to win for his cause a commander who could validly oppose with his artillery department the fall into enemy hands of an important airport, he did not hesitate to engage in an unequal bitter fight of which he was the ardent animator, but in the hard fight fell shot dead. While he exhaled, after excruciating agony, his last breath, he perfected that surrender that in his fine intuition had to be rejected at any cost. With his supreme sacrifice he marked the luminous path of duty and honor to most people. - Tirana, 13 September 1943* ".

The 5th Squadron of the II Squadron Group "Cavalleggeri Guide" was reached on 9 September by the news that the Tirana airport was in danger of being occupied by the Germans, but on 12 September,

35 The battery had to sell 7 CL39 trucks, 4 two-seater Benelli motorcycles and a FIAT 1100 car to the French departments.

surrounded by units of the 100. Jäger-Divison in their barracks in the near Skumbini, he gave up his weapons at around 21:00.
The "Cavalleggeri di Monferrato" Regiment, commanded by Colonel Luigi Lanzuolo and which had 30 L6 / 40 tanks, was also stationed in Albania, in the Berat area, on the Osum river, at the foot of Mount Tomori, and also depended on it from the 9th Army of General Renzo Dalmazzo. The Regimental Command and the 1st Squadron Group, together with other Italian forces, garrisoned the city of Berat and the surroundings, while the 2nd Squadron Group, commanded by Major Pietro Carbone, was detached in the Devoli oil basin to safeguard the interests Italians represented there by AIPA (Italian Company Petroli Albanesi). Already in the aftermath of the Armistio, requests from the Germans began to reach Major Carbone, asking to surrender their weapons and free the defense posts, placed to guard the oil wells. On 13 September a German truck unit attempted a surprise attack on the Devoli garrison, promptly rejected thanks to the energetic reaction of Major Carbone, who had ordered the 3rd and 4th Squadrons to return fire. On 18 September, Colonel Lanzuolo went with the 1st Squadron Group along the Berat - Lushnja roadway, a few kilometers as the crow flies from Devoli. The following day, Colonel Lanzuolo reported to the officers of the 2nd Group, communicating that no more orders had been received from the superior commands and that he considered the offer made by the Germans to reach the Bitolj railway station in Yugoslavia as a trap. to then continue under their control towards Italy. Major Carbone, who had already consulted the officers of the 2nd Group, expressed his intention not to allow disarmament by the Germans and mentioned that he had had some contacts with partisan leaders in the area. On the 21st Lanzuolo made an agreement with Vangel Zoto, one of the most influential Communist partisan leaders in the area, for the passage of the "Monferrato" Regiment to the local Resistance. From this moment the soldiers of the Regiment were gradually disarmed by the Albanian partisans, to be then assigned to different units, in order to avoid that an Italian unit remained united, disciplined and above all armed, although inserted in the resistance device. At the beginning of October, for a short period, Colonel Lanzuolo was also, in fact, a prisoner of the partisan commands, as he was imprisoned as a "guest" in the fortress of Berat. On 20 October the "Monferrato" Regiment was definitively dissolved, with all its effective aggregates, in small groups, with different partisan departments. At dawn on November 15, 1943, Berat was hit by a massive German attack, which overwhelmed the partisans. Mechanized units, preceded by low-altitude strafing and supported by a few wagons, quickly prevailed over the defense of the Albanian partisan forces. Colonel Lanzuolo was taken prisoner by the Germans during the round-up that followed the fight and was shot near Berat the same day. The Gold Medal for Military Valor was granted to his memory with the following motivation: "*Soldier of pure temperament, skilled and shrewd commander, he assumed the command of the" Cavalleggeri Monferrato "regiment in Albania by his express wish, keeping its moral compactness , the spirit of daring, attachment to the distant homeland and to duty through the difficult events and the dangerous political situation of that land. After the armistice, with his vigilant command action, he managed to free the entire regiment from capture by taking it to the mountain in defense of freedom and justice. Attacked, after a strenuous fight always in the midst and example of his cavalrymen, taken prisoner he was brutally slaughtered by the Germans. He was thus making a holocaust of his life for wanting to keep faith in his honor as a soldier and commander. his sacrifice served as an example to his cavalrymen who were able to avenge his memory by fighting compactly in the ranks of the patriots-Berat (Albania), March-15 November 1943*"[36]. His Cavalrymen, following the directives left by the commander, unable to continue the fight as an organic unit, went into hiding fighting in the partisan formations. The Regiment was no longer reconstituted.

36 Lanzuolo had also fought in the Great War, during which he was decorated with the Bronze Medal for Military Valor (Castelnuovo, September 1915) and the War Cross for Military Valor (Bainsizza, August 1917); by Royal Decree of April 18, 1931 he was also appointed Knight of the Order of the Crown of Italy.

8. Balcans

At the time of the Armistice in the Balkans there were many Italian armored units, scattered over a vast territory. The situation of the armored units was as follows:

- From the 11th Army Corps, with headquarters in Ljubljana, depended:
  - Autonomous Company Carri in Zadar
  - Armored Car Company in Ljubljana
  - I Battalion of the 31st Tank Infantry Regiment (dependent on the "Lombardia" Division) with the 2nd Company in Jastrebarsko, the 3rd Company in Cronomelj and the 2nd Flamethrower Company
- from the V Corps, with headquarters in Crikvenica, depended:
  - 1st Group L Tanks Group "San Giusto"
- from the 13th Army Corps, divided between Split and Zadar, depended:
  - Tank Battalion of the 1st Division "Celere" in Split (the Division had moved to Sussak, but its units were still located between Split and Knin)
- from the VI Army Corps, with headquarters in Dubrovnik, depended:
  - II Tank Group
- from the 14th Army Corps in Montenegro depended:
  - III Battalion of the 31st Tank Infantry Regiment.

The L tank companies present in the Balkans found themselves unable to return to the Motherland, and they dissolved practically without attempting any resistance, abandoning their tanks and armored cars, often without sabotaging them, which ended up in the hands of the Germans and the Tito partisans. . The Germans, on the other hand, were already ready for an eventual Italian defection from August, fearing above all a collapse of Northern Italy and Italian Slovenia, easy access points to the Reich from the south. In Ljubljana on 9 September, the day after the armistice, the 19.SS-Polizei Regiment disarmed the XI Army Corps in Ljubljana and the Division "Hunters of the Alps" and took possession of numerous armored vehicles AB41 and self-protected AS37, which they went to integrate the armored vehicles of the Aufkl.Abt.17.

In this climate of defeat, one of the few exceptions was represented by the II Carri Group "San Marco". In fact, on 13 September in Dubrovnik the 2nd and 3rd Squadrons quickly organized a resistance against the SS Division "Prinz Eugen", which had reached the city, engaging in a furious fight, which lasted for a few hours and, despite the fierce defense , the Italian troops were forced to surrender and numerous L3 tanks and some ancient Lancia 1ZM armored cars were confiscated by the German military.

In Split, where a squadron of the II "San Marco" Tank Group was located, General Becuzzi, commander of the 15th "Bergamo" Division, but also the highest civil authority of the city, held an ambivalent attitude when on 10 September the Slavic partisans made the their entry into the city: on the one hand he showed his desire to come to terms with the Titoites, on the other he tried to make contact and to negotiate with the German armed forces. The Slavic partisans soon discovered this double game and took possession of Italian weapons and equipment by force, fearing that the latter would not oppose any attacks conducted by the Germans, also capturing the 16 tanks between L3 and L6 and at least 2 armored car AB41, which formed the armored equipment of the squadron of the "San Marco" Group present in the city.

Three units instead decided to continue the war alongside the German armed forces.

In Montenegro, the III Battalion of the 31st Tank Regiment was reached in Podgorica with the news of the Armistice, signed on 8 September in Cassibile. In the climate of general uncertainty, on 10 September Captain Ripandelli, commander of the 6th Company, with the subordinate officers, gathered the unit and, flanked by officers of the 5th Company and of the Battalion Command Company, gave a speech in which he declared that for the good of the Fatherland it was necessary to remain alongside the Germans and continue the war, thus asking those who wanted to continue fighting to take a step forward. Almost all the personnel of the 6th Company adhered without hesitation to the proposal of Captain Ripandelli. In the evening, the 6th Company, together with some Tankmen from the other Companies who had also decided to continue fighting alongside the German troops, moved to the clearing where the Wehrmacht units were set aside. The soldiers and the tanks were thus framed in 118. Jäger-Division, in Podgorica and in the following days some Italian soldiers disbanded by other Weapons showed up at the camp of the company, asking to be able to join: the Germans immediately prepared bilingual cards dated 9 September 1943 and therefore began the collaboration with the Germanic departments. From that moment the L3 wagons of the department received a particular distinctive sign, a Balkenkreuz with double white corners on the sides of the casemates, and on the rear edges there were white progressive Arabic numerals on a light-colored rectangle, which replaced the old distinctive number of the Regiment . These were the only signs that identified the collaboration between the former allies, given that the tank crews kept the gray-green uniform, insignia and individual and unit armament. In November, some L tanks participated in counter-guerrilla operations with German units and in December a platoon participated in a round-up action, which ended with the loss of 2 tanks, with casualties and injuries. After this operation, the L wagons, while always remaining ready and available for use, remained stationary at the parking lots and were no longer used. Between the end of January and the beginning of February 1944, the order came to leave Podgorica to fall back on the Müsingen field in Germany, with the aim of setting up an armored battalion for the 1st Assault Division, a department which, however, did not was never established. The Tankers who with their charismatic company commander had detached themselves from the 31st Tank Regiment thus went to form the logistic battalion of the "Monterosa" Alpine Division of the Army of the Social Republic in the meantime established in northern Italy.

In Montenegro there was also the XL Bersaglieri Battalion of the 5th Regiment, whose 1st Company, equipped with armored vehicles, passed with the German armed forces.

The "San Giusto" Tank Group I was a rather inefficient unit, equipped with about forty tanks worn by long use, with the squadrons located as follows:

- Command, Command Squadron and Workshop in Susak
- 1st Squadron in Ogulin and Delnice
- 2nd Squadron in Susak and Crikvenica
- 3rd Squadron in Rijeka, Karlobag and Vratnik
- 4th Squadron in Kristanje and Perkovic.

The departments present in Rijeka remained compact at the announcement of the Armistice, but in the following days many soldiers left the Group, until the commander ordered its dissolution, shortly before the arrival of the Germans in the city. In the meantime, the men of the 1st Squadron had arrived in the city, now disbanded, who had been disarmed by Yugoslav partisans along the way. The 3rd Squadron reached Rijeka on September 14th together with the "Murge" Division and in all probability disbanded. The 4th Squadron, which was in the Zadar area, probably surrendered to the 114th Jäger-Division without a fight, together with the other units located there. The fate of the 2nd Light

Tank Squadron, commanded by Captain Agostino Tonegutti, was different. In the days immediately following the Armistice, a handful of men reached Fiume with about fifteen L3 wagons. After having contributed to the defense of the city, on German orders, the "San Giusto" first moved to Gorizia (February 1944), where its staff were reinforced and received armored and wheeled vehicles from the Germanic Armed Forces, and finally to Mariano del Friuli (GO), in April of the same year. The department, renamed the "San Giusto" Armored Squadrons Group, was structured on Command, Command Squadron, M Tank Squadron and L Tank Squadron, with a maximum endowment of 35 armored vehicles of various types, all of Italian production, and a staff that reached the 130 units. The tasks entrusted to the unit were escorting logistic and military convoys in general, support for anti-partisan actions especially in support of German units, patrolling the communication routes and, occasionally, the inhabited centers in the Goriziano, eastern Friuli and western Karst . The department disbanded in Mariano del Friuli on 27 April 1945, after an operational department of the Group had taken part in the days preceding an attempted counter-offensive in the Rupa area (now in Croatia).

9. Aegean

The Armistice signed by the Badoglio government and made known to the Armed Forces on 8 September 1943 also took by surprise the Italian troops stationed in the so-called "Italian Aegean islands", essentially the Dodecanese, where the "Regina Division" was stationed as garrison. ", under whose dependence was the CCCXII Mixed Tank Battalion[37]. At the time of the Armistice, the Battalion had only 2 L Tank Companies and was waiting to receive, from Italy, the third Company equipped with M tanks. It was the 15th Tank Company of the Depot of the 3rd Tank Infantry Regiment of Bologna, which, should have been equipped with M wagons and should have been sent to the Dodecanese, in July 1943, but the transfer did not take place due to the evolution of war events. The armored unit did not take part in the clashes against the German troops that took place on the island as early as the evening of 8 September, unlike other Italian units present in the archipelago, but on 9 September the crews of the Lancia armored cars blocked their vehicles along the road to Rhodes and set them on fire, lest they fall into German hands. The Battalion was thus dissolved on 11 September, after the surrender of all the Italian units to the German Square Command in Rhodes. A part of the Tankers, however, asked and obtained to be able to continue hostilities alongside the Germans and with the tanks present on the island of Rhodes, presumably no more than a dozen, an Armored Company was formed, with a staff of 1 officer and 135 non-commissioned officers. and enlisted men. The Company was attached to the "Italian Rhodes Regiment" ("Italienisch Rhodos Regiment"), part of the Sturmdivision Rhodos. The Regiment did not take part in firefights due to lack of enemies, mainly carried out police duties and surrendered, with the German garrison of the island of Rhodes, on 5 May 1945 to the Allies.

Similarly, in Crete, at the time of the Armistice, there were 6 L3 tanks, which remained on the island after the "Merkur" operation, framed in the 51st Autonomous Company L3, organized after the occupation of the island with men and vehicles of the CCCXII Mixed Tank Battalion. While the Ger

---

37 Born as the L tank battalion in May 1939 within the 31st Tank Infantry Regiment, it was transferred to the Aegean on March 30, 1940, based in Psito, on the island of Rhodes. During its stay on the island, a Section of 2 old Lancia 1ZM armored cars of the Royal Carabinieri Cyclists Company, a Platoon of 4 Lancia 1ZM of the Royal Army, which had already been on the island since the 1930s, passed to his dependence, and the 3rd Frontier Tank Company L5, better known as FIAT 3000, transferred to the Dodecanese in mid 1940. The Battalion was not involved in any war action, as the archipelago was only marginally affected by war events. The only exception was the occupation of Crete, known by the code name of "Operation Merkur" (20 - 31 May 1941), in which the 3rd Company of the CCCXII Mixed Tank Battalion with 13 L3 tanks took part, which performed the function of scouting group of Italian troops.

mans occupied the entire island, the CLXI "M" Blackshirt Assault Battalion immediately sided with the Germanic armed forces and thus the "Italian Legion of Crete Volunteers" was formed, under the command of Lieutenant Colonel Gianoli. The Legion, with the 6 tanks present on the island, managed to set up an armored unit (51st Tank Platoon), which was stationed in Retymno, with a force of 22 men. The Platoon, which was formally part of the Republican National Guard, faced some enemy attacks from the sea and, above all, from the air, also suffering the inconveniences related to isolation and scarcity of food, laying down their weapons on May 4, 1945, together to German units.

▲ General Ercole Calvi, commander of the 32nd Tank Regiment in Sardinia, found himself having to face the difficult situation created on the island and in Corsica, with 11 battalions and groups under him.

▲ Balancing exercises for a L3 / 33, probably from the 2nd L Tank Battalion, in Sardinia (D'Alessandro)

▼ The crew of a L3 / 33 light tank of the II Tank Battalion L35 in front of their tank (D'Alessandro).

▲ German armored vehicles in Palau in Sardinia in the days following the Armistice (B.A.).

▼ Officers of the German armored units in conversation in Palau, waiting to move following the announcement of the Italian Armistice (B.A.).

▲ A L3 / 33 light tank in Sardinia (D'Alessandro).

▼ Disembarkation of 47/32 self-propelled vehicles in the port of Bastia on 11 November 1942.

▲ Close-up of the same chariot in the previous photograph, which allows you to see the tactical symbol painted on the bow of the vehicle (D'Alessandro).

▲ Another 47/32 self-propelled vehicle from the CXXXI L40 Self-propelled Battalion lands in Bastia.

▼ Italian L3 tanks on the Ajaccio seafront in Corsica (Benvenuti - Colonna).

▲ Italian armored cars in an inhabited center of Corsica.

▼ On the Place d'Austerlitz in Ajaccio, in front of the monument dedicated to Napoleon Bonaparte, some Italian L3 / 33 tanks of the 13th L Tank Battalion parade. The vehicle in the foreground is entirely painted in dark green (Manes).

▲ Italian armored cars in Avenue Jean Nicoli in Corte, in north-central Corsica, a town where the Italian command of the island was located.

▼ Armored and motorcyclists of the Bersaglieri of the 10th Raggruppamento Celere escort a column through the streets of an inhabited center in Corsica, near an Italian checkpoint, reinforced with road interruptions, made with dry stone walls.

▲ Armored car AB41 of the Bersaglieri of the 7th Company Car armored car of the 10th Raggruppamento Celere driving near the town from the town of Corte, whose historic center can be seen in the background on the right. The machines have snow chains on the bow.

▲ Wehrmacht officers interviewed during the boarding operations for Corsica in Palau on 8 September 1943 (B.A.).

▼ German vehicles of the 90th Panzergrenadier-Division departing from Sardinia, where they will join the soldiers of the SS-Sturmbrigade "Reichsführer SS", with the aim of ousting the Italian armed forces and taking over the island (B.A.).

▲ A tank officer scans the horizon with binoculars from an L3 / 33 Radio in Corsica; it can be seen that the wagon has been brought to CV38 standards, thanks to the presence of battery boxes on the front fenders (Arena).

▼ CV38 tanks in Corsica parked in front of a school. The first tank, an L3 / 38 Radio with whip antenna, bears the tank crew's metal emblem on the front of the tank and has reddish brown and black camouflage and spots on a green background (Arena).

▲ Mass at the camp officiated among the 47/32 self-propelled vehicles in Corsica (Crippa).

▼ A column of self-propelled vehicles of the CXXXI Self-propelled Battalion L40 marching through the Corsican hills.

▲ The same column in the previous photo crosses a built-up area. The vehicle in the lead is a self-propelled command, equipped with radio equipment; all self-propelled machines have a uniform sand yellow color.

▼ Self-propelled Stu.G. III of the SS-Sturmbrigade "Reichsführer SS" move from Bastia to the ports of San Bonifacio and Porto Vecchio, where the units of the 90.Panzergrenadier-Division would have landed (Arena).

Soldati e Marinai Italiani !

Dopo aver seminato sull'Italia la desolazione e la distruzione, Mussolini è vilmente fuggito davanti il furore popolare e i colpi degli Alleati. Un vento di liberazione percorre la penisola. Ma si vuol continuare a farvi servire Hitler.

VOI NON ACCETTERETE!

I vostri fratelli in Italia non accettano.

A Roma, a Milano, a Torino, delle enormi folle gridano: LA LIBERTA E LA PACE. I tedeschi occupano Trieste e Fiume.

A Milano, a Napoli a Torino, i tedéschi sparano sulle vostre donne e sui vostri bambini.

Nessuno puo ormai soffocare le aspirazioni profonde del Popolo italiano.

Soldati e Marinai !

Solo l'armistizio mette fine agli orrori della guerra e vi permette di ritornare a casa.

Liberato la Patria vostra dalla rapacità tedesca. Guerra al Nazismo, in Corsica come altrove.

Accogliete gli Alleati come liberatori.

DIVENITE COMBATTENTI DELLA LIBERTA.

Solo a questa condizione salverete la vastra vita e il vostro onore.

IL FRONTE NAZIONALE CORSO

▲ The Corsican National Front, after the Italian Armistice, carried out a media bombing of the Italian soldiers, urging them to join the local Resistance against the Germans, through persuasive posters and leaflets.

▲ Italian armored vehicles guard the Boulevard Dominique Paoli in Bastia, after the announcement of the Armistice.

▼ A 47/32 L40 self-propelled machine of the XX 47/32 Self-propelled Battalion guards the port of Bastia in Corsica, after the Italian troops had recaptured it from the German soldiers; the vehicle has a "RE 5720" plate; in the background the damaged steamer "Humanitas" (Arena).

▲After a night of fighting, the port of Bastia, occupied by German troops only for a few hours, was resumed thanks to the decisive Italian intervention, supported by the self-propelled vehicles of the XX Battalion.

THE (FAILURE) RECONSTITUTION OF THE TANKER SPECIALTY IN THE SO-CALLED "SOUTHERN KINGDOM"

The announcement of the Armistice caused the dissolution of most of the armored units of the Royal Army, as we have seen previously. Already in September 1943, however, the slow process of reconstitution of the Royal Army began, when on September 26 the First Motorized Group was formed near Lecce, in San Pietro Vernotico. The Group, commanded by General Vincenzo Dapino, who was succeeded by General Umberto Utili, included elements of the 58th Legnano Infantry Division. On 3 December, attached to the 36th American "Texas" Division, he participated in the breakthrough of the Bernhardt Line at Montelungo, with bloody losses and above all a high number of missing people. The Group managed to conquer Montelungo on the following December 16, managing to impress the Allies, who did not put their trust in this Italian department.

On 8 October 1943, General Umberto Utili drew up a document which estimated the number of armored vehicles that could be made available for the Royal Army, in view of a reorganization and entry into the war alongside the Allies. In particular, the General assumed that 60 M wagons, 75 self-propelled 75, 60 L and 40 self-propelled 47 wagons could be fielded, numbers that were then reduced due to any losses suffered by the units in Corsica, which were not yet Note. Among these numbers were considered the tanks present in Sardinia, where however the Allies, considering the use of Italian troops on the island now useless, had ordered a census of the artillery materials present, from which they were available, probably in view of a probable alienation:

- 80 FIAT 35 8 mm machine guns for L3 tank
- 224 Breda 38 8 mm machine guns per tank
- 32 7.35 mm machine guns for Somua tank
- 6 12.7 mm machine guns for L35 tank
- 36 guns per Somua tank
- 12 47/32 guns for M tank
- 40 guns of 47/40 for M tank[38]
- 69 75/18 guns for self-propelled.

On 24 September 1943, the Allics had also had the radio stations in Sardinia delivered and the equipment on board the wagons sealed, making it impossible for the armored units to maneuver.

On April 18, 1944 the First Motorized Group, with about 22,000 men, took the name of the Italian Liberation Corps, organized into two Divisions, the "Nembo" and the "Utili", the latter formed by what had been the First Motorized Grouping and other departments. The CIL entered the line on the Adriatic front at the beginning of June, under the command of General Umberto Utili, fighting alongside the Polish army. The armored vehicles surveyed by General Utili could have equipped the Italian Corps of Liberation, together with some vehicles recovered in Rome after the arrival of the Anglo-Americans[39], but, with the exception of a section of 3 AB41 armored cars of the IX Assault Battalion, the C.I.L. it was not equipped with any armored department and was disbanded on 24 September 1944, when the formation of 6 units at the divisional level, called Combat Groups, began.

38 Mounted on M15 / 42.

39 It consisted of 1 M13 / 40 wagon, 1 self-propelled 74, two self-propelled 105 and an armored car, recovered from the Motorization Research Center, and 8 armored cars of the Italian Africa Police.

The birth of these Groups, however, definitively put the word "end" to the ambitions of being able to reconstitute Italian co-belligerent armored units. In fact, the six autonomous Combat Groups ("Cremona", "Legnano", "Friuli", "Mantova", "Piceno" and "Folgore") were each comparable to a light Division, but without an armored component. The Infantry units of the Groups were assigned in large numbers only the Universal Carrier MKI and MKII armored treads, according to the standard equipment provided for the British Infantry battalions, while all mortar units were mounted on Mortar Carriers.

The Allies therefore proved wary, as much as the Germans towards the Social Republic, of the reconstruction of Italian armored military units to be used against the Germanic Armed Forces.

10. 32nd and 132nd Tank Regiment

In Sardinia, where the presence of tanks was greater, there was a progressive relegation of tank units to secondary tasks, destined in fact to oblivion. After the Germans were expelled from the island, the Raggruppamento Motocorazzato on 9 October 1943 was ordered to fall back on Cagliari, to return to the continent, but then remained stationed in the area. The 32nd Tank Regiment, which had been dissolved on 2 October 1943, was reconstituted on 13 March 1944 by the 132nd Tank Regiment, organized on:

- 1st M Tank Battalion
- 2nd M Tank Battalion
- 3rd Somua Tank Battalion
- 4th Motorcyclists Battalion
- 5th 75/28 Self-propelled Guns Group.

In May the 32nd and 132nd Regiments were placed in the reconstituted "Grenadiers of Sardinia" Division, resulting, in fact, the only two tank units of the Royal Army at that date.

The 32nd Tank Regiment was organized on:

- 1st M Tank Battalion
- 2nd M Tank Battalion
- 3rd L Tank Battalion.

The 132nd Tank Regiment, on the other hand, had this structure:

- 1st L Tank Battalion
- 2nd L Tank Battalion
- 3rd 47/32 Self-propelled Guns Battalion
- 4th 47/32 Self-propelled Guns Battalion.

These units had no operational use, due to the open hostility of the Anglo-Americans, and they were instead ordered to be dissolved on 31 August 1944 by the Military Command of Sardinia. All the tanks were concentrated in Guspini, under the direction of the 13th Automobile Park, thus decreeing the end of the Tanker specialty of the Royal Army.

11. 5th L Flamethrower Tank Company

In the staff of the 1st Motorized Group, the 5th Flamethrower Company was foreseen, which in the intentions should have been part of the V Counter-tank Battalion, together with 2 47/32 Counter-tank Companies. The Company, however, did not join the group, probably due to the prohibition of the Allied authorities, and was deployed in Monterosi (LE), with a fleet of 12 L3 / 35LF wagons.

Two tanks were seconded to the "Piceno" Division, where they were used for the anti-tank training of the Arditi of the "Duca d'Aosta" Battalion of the Regia Aeronautica and were available for the training of tank officers of the Regia Accademia di Lecce. The Company was then transferred to Taranto, where it carried out tasks of public order and where it was dissolved on 2 October 1944.

12. 1051th Battalion "Autieri Carristi"

The LI Tank Battalion was set up within the LI Corps on 15 September 1943, a department which, however, had a very short life. The Battalion, whose mobilization began on 1 October 1943, had a particular organic constitution, due to the scarce availability of men and means:

- Command
- 1st Tanker Company (on foot)
- 2nd Tanker Company (on foot)
- L Flamethrower Tank Company (probably without tanks)

The unit was renamed 1051th Battalion "Autieri Carristi" in February 1944 and was located in Salice Salentino (LE). The unit, framed in the Italian Armed Forces Group, then provided, from June 1944, logistical support to the British 8th Army, recovering and repairing tanks directly on the front line, until the end of the conflict..

13. Cavalry Squadron - IX Assault Battalion

This was the only small armored unit present within the Italian Liberation Corps: it was the Exploring Section, consisting only of 3 AB41 armored cars, assigned to the Cavalry Squadron, which constituted one of the four Companies of the IX Assault Battalion " Col Moschin "from 5 July 1944. The armored cars took part in the attack conducted by the IX Assault Battalion for the forcing of the Musone river on 17 July. After the offensive in the Gubbio area (17 August), the General Staff of the Royal Army attempted to remedy the problem of the inadequacy of the resources needed to counter the enemy tanks by proposing to create an armored core with means of national production. The 3 AB41 armored cars supplied to the IX Assault Department should have been joined by others, perhaps 6, 1 M and 3 self-propelled tanks of 75 and 105[40]. The development of events (on 30 August 1944 the C.I.L. was dissolved), however, made this proposal late. The IX Assault Battalion was dissolved in Brescia in the second half of 1945[41].

14. "F" Squadron

Established in early December 1944 by Captain Carlo Francesco Gay, and dependent on the 6th British Armored Division, with a staff of 130 paratroopers from the 3rd and 11th Battalions of the 154th "Nembo" Regiment, the "Folgore" Reconnaissance Squadron it was equipped with its own fleet, supplemented by an armored car platoon, made up of four AB41s. On March 12, 1944, two armored cars of the Squadron competed for the occupation of Montenerodomo (CH), a location used as a base for the reconnaissance of the department. At the beginning of June, a vanguard made up of two Platoons of Paratroopers and two AB41 armored cars occupied Isola del Liri (FR). During the summer, the "F" Squadron was deprived of its armored cars, which were sold to the Command of the Italian Liberation Corps.

---

40 These were, in all likelihood, the vehicles recovered in Rome and mentioned above, while part of the armored cars were those already in charge, as we will see later, by the "F" Squadron.

41 Also elements of the 4th L "San Marco" Tank Squadron Group were aggregated to the IX Assault Battalion, but without armored vehicles.

▲ On the way to Bastia, the wreck of a German self-propelled Stug. III Ausf. G of the SS-Sturmbrigade "Reichsführer SS", destroyed by Italian artillery, is inspected by the Royal Army's health troops (Arena).

▼ Soldiers of an Italian health department are preparing to collaborate with departments of the French degaullista, arrived in Corsica from North Africa (Arena).

▲ A French officer of the forces loyal to De Gaulle studies a map together with an officer of the XX Self-Propelled Battalion and one of the "Friuli" Division in Corsica.

▲ German artillery concentrated in the proto of Bastia, awaiting embarkation, to leave Corsica (Arena).

▼ German vehicles are hastily loaded onto the canal after the defeat in Corsica (Arena).

▲ A self-propelled L40 from 47/32 that has been renovated (with some poetic license) and kept at the Musée de la Résistance Corse in Zonza, a village in the Alta Rocca in Corsica.

▼ In the days following the Armistice, in the Balkans, to identify the Italian tanks that were collaborating with the German Armed Forces, the crews painted flashy white rectangular markings on the vehicles. On this CV33, in movement together with Germanic departments, the system of markings is evident, painted on the monochromatic livery, probably gray-green (B.A.).

▲ Lieutenant Colonel Luigi Goytre, commander of the IV Armored Group of the "Cavalleggeri di Vittorio Emanuele II" Regiment, fell fighting against the Germans in Tirana on 13 September 1943, in an attempt to defend the city's airport.

▲ Colonel Luigi Lanzuolo, commander of the "Cavalleggeri di Monferrato" Armored Group in a photograph from 1938. In memory of the Colonel, killed in Albania by the Germans after 8 September, for leading his men against the Germanic armed forces , the Gold Medal for Military Valor was awarded.

I carristi del III Battaglione continuano a combattere

Al Duce dell'Italia repubblicana fascista è pervenuto il seguente telegramma:

« Gli ufficiali, sottufficiali e i carristi usciti dalla file del III battaglione carri, schieratisi con i loro carri al fianco dei camerati tedeschi fin dall'11 settembre, esultano di poter continuare a combattere ai Vostri ordini per la liberazione e la grandezza della Patria immortale. Vinceremo! - F.to: Comando 118° battaglione carri della 218.a Divisione alpini tedesca. Il comandante capitano: *Ulrico Ripandelli* ».

▲Text of the telegram sent by Captain Ripandelli, commander of the 6th Company of the III Battalion of the 31st Tank Regiment, to Benito Mussolini, to express the will of his unit to continue the war alongside the Germans, after the Armistice. The telegram reads: *"The officers, non-commissioned officers and tankers who left the ranks of the III Tank Battalion, lined up with their tanks alongside the German comrades since September 11, rejoice in being able to fight under your orders for the liberation and greatness of the Fatherland immortal. We will win!" (Pisanò).*

TANKERS IN THE RESISTANCE

After the Armistice, many Italian soldiers chose, for various reasons, to go into hiding and to contribute to the War of Liberation in a clandestine manner, joining the partisan movements. The Tankers also participated in the resistance movement, but never succeeded in establishing an organic formation, but only individually, or in organizing armored units, for obvious reasons[42].

Probably a unique exception was the Garibaldi band commanded by "Francino", aka Lieutenant Francesco Tumiati of the 32nd Tank Regiment. After deciding to go into hiding to fight the Germans, towards the end of 1943, he reached the Marches, followed by a group of tank crews employed by him, and became commander of the "Pisacane" detachment of the Garibaldi "Pesaro" Brigade. In January 1944, after the tragic bombing of Urbania (PU), Tumiati went to the town to help the population, regardless of the risk of being arrested as a reluctant, and did his utmost in removing the rubble, in the unearthing of the bodies, in providing assistance. and transportation of the wounded. Known for his daring actions to the detriment of the Germanic armed forces, "Francino" led his tankmen for eight months until his capture, which took place in May 1944, during a massive roundup. "Francino" was subjected by the Germans to a summary trial, during which he was urged to betray his comrades in exchange for his own safety, but he refused any compromise and was shot at the cemetery of Cantiano (PU) together with them, the Yugoslavs Djuro Franisić (sometimes referred to as Giuro Kuzeta) and Batrić Bulatović[43].

At least two tankmen were shot in the Fosse Ardeatine on March 24, 1944, precisely for their anti-fascist militancy: the Second Lieutenant Saverio Coen (of Jewish origin, collaborated with the British secret services) and the Carrista Gaetano Butera[44]. Saverio Coen, of Jewish origin, had participated in the Abyssinian Campaign, but, in 1938, following the enactment of the racial laws, he was forced to change his identity and obtain false documents; during the German occupation of the capital he collaborated with the British secret services, until his arrest in January 1944. Gaetano Butera was in service in the 4th Tank Regiment and participated in the defense of Rome, fighting against the German troops. After the German occupation, Butera joined the partisan organization "Armed bands of Lazio", finally being arrested during an ambush.

It is necessary to remember the charismatic figure of Alfredo di Dio. Famous fencing champion, Alfredo, after having attended the Academy of Modena, was appointed Lieutenant in Effective Permanent Service of the 1st Tank Infantry Regiment. On 8 September, while he was being transferred from Vercelli to Novara, after having unsuccessfully presented himself to the commander of this square to propose to him to organize a resistance to the Germans, he moved towards the mountains

42 The case of the Tito partisans was different, who were able to form real armored units, both with material captured from the Italians after the Armistice, and with armored vehicles supplied by the Allies. Among the Slavic partisans there were also Tankers of the dissolved Royal Army, who opted to join the Communist resistance, who often managed to bring with them even a small number of tanks.

43 For this he was decorated with the Gold Medal for Military Valor: "*Arrived as a simple partisan in the ranks of a Garibaldi Brigade, he reached the rank of detachment commander for demonstrated value. Brave to the point of temerity and sustained by ardent faith even in the most difficult moments, he never wavered in the face of danger and, after having strenuously endured for 18 days the bloody pressure of a powerful German round-up, he fell into the hands of the enemy. Subjected to quick judgment, he maintained the fiercest demeanor and, disdainfully refusing to have his life saved at the cost of cowardly betrayal, confronted the firing squad with the serenity of heroes, offering his chest to the enemy lead who cut off his bold youth. - Cantiano (Pesaro), May 17, 1944* ".

44 Second Lieutenant Saverio Coen was decorated with a Silver Medal for Military Valor in memory, while Tanker Gaetano Butera with a Gold Medal for Military Valor in memory.

between the Novarese and Ossola areas and, after a clash with the Germans, he went into hiding with a group of his soldiers. Joined by his brother Antonio, he joined the "Patrioti Valstrona" Brigade in Val d'Ossola. He reorganized his men and first constituted the "Filippo Beltrami" Alpine Assault Brigade and then the "Val Toce" Division, formations of Catholic inspiration, assuming command with the battle name "Marco". Among the most important autonomous Catholic-oriented formations, the "Val Toce", which was one of the largest autonomous partisan units of Catholic inspiration and which came to frame 22,000 partisans scattered between Piedmont and Lombardy, distinguished itself above all in the battle for the liberation 'Ossola. During the clashes in the Ossola area, Di Dio died during a violent firefight in Val Cannobina, where massive German units were pressing, on 12 October 1944. A Gold Medal for Military Valor was awarded to his memory.[45].

Finally, we recall what happened in Rome, where personnel of the dissolved 4th Tank Regiment were framed in the aforementioned Mobile Public Security Battalion of the Republican Police. Many of these tankers of the 4th secretly joined patriotic organizations in the capital, which were headed by Lieutenant Colonel Luigi Battisti, former commander of one of the battalions of the dissolved Regiment, acting as infiltrated informants. We remember in particular the aforementioned Lieutenant Tanker Raffaello Parri, who was the standard bearer of the 4th Tank Regiment. After the Armistice he kept the banner of the Regiment, hiding it in the house until the end of the conflict, saving it from certain end. Having entered the Roman Resistance, he too infiltrated the Rome Police, thus being able to have valuable information, which allowed the lives of partisans and Jews to be saved. Parri, who learned of the attack in via Rasella, hid in a convent for several months, fearing being discovered and captured[46].

---

45 *"Army officer in s.p.e., from the first day of the resistance he was at the head of his own unit in the fierce battle against the oppressor. He organized the first partisan groups and with magnificent courage led them into the unequal struggle through a series of daring exploits. Captured by the enemy, with disdainful pride he underwent harsh interrogations and, having managed to free himself, recklessly resumed his fighting post by participating in the operations that, through long months of bloody struggle, led to the conquest of the Vai d'Ossola. In this first strip of Italy valiantly conquered he resisted for forty days with his men exhausted, hungry and poorly armed against enemy forces of overwhelming superiority, until with weapons in hand he met heroic death at the head of his partisans. - Strona Valley, September 1943; Ossola Valley, Val Vigezzo, Finero, September - October 1944".*

46 In fact, Colonel Montezemolo, who directed the clandestine formations which also included the tankers of the 4th Carristi, was one of the victims of the Fosse Ardeatine.

▲ Elements of the 6th Company of the III Battalion of the 31st Tank Regiment, commanded by Captain Ulrico Ripandelli, continued to fight alongside the Germans of the 118. Jager - Division after the Armistice. A particular system of insignia was placed on the tanks, consisting of a peculiar Balkenkreuz and a progressive numbering (B.A.).

▼ The "San Giusto" Armored Squadron Group was organized after the Armistice with cavalry units of the dissolved Royal Army, which had refused the change of front and decided to continue the war alongside the German armed forces. In this photo a L3 / 33 of the Group taken in the courtyard of the Industrial School of Mariano del Friuli (GO), headquarters of the department, in autumn 1944. The coat of arms of the department is painted on the shield of the machine guns in its latest version with the tricolor waving, while on the sides of the casemate there are still the tactical symbols of the Royal Army (Benvenuti - Colonna).

▲ An L3 tank of the CCCXII Mixed Tank Battalion embarks before leaving for Crete, occupied by the Italian-German forces, during the "Merkur" operation between 20 and 31 May 1941.

▼ The tankers of the CCCXII Mixed Tank Battalion of the Aegean, unsuccessfully tried to sabotage their Lancia 1ZM armored cars by setting them on fire along the road to Rhodes on September 9, 1943. Although now obsolete, the armored cars were stripped by German soldiers, who went to the place to inspect them, everything that can be reused, such as machine guns, ammunition and tires. The busway in the foreground is labeled "RE 88B" and you can hardly notice the curious camouflage pattern with small yellowish patches, probably brush-painted on the uniform dark green color.

▲ Lieutenant Francesco Tumiati of the 32nd Tank Regiment. After 8 September he organized, with a group of his tankers, a partisan nucleus, becoming with the name of "Francino", commander of the "Pisacane" detachment of the Garibaldi "Pesaro" Brigade. He died in May 1944, after being captured by the Germans during a massive roundup, being decorated with a Gold Medal for Military Valor in his memory.

▲ The units of the "co-belligerent" Royal Army did not receive any armored vehicles, if not a large number of British cradles, sufficient for the logistical needs of the units. In this photo a Universal Carrier MK II of the CLXXXV Arditi Paratroopers "Nembo" Department of the Italian Liberation Corps in L'Aquila on June 16, 1944 (Ricchezza).

▼ The only three AB41 armored cars in the AB40 section of the IX Assault Department of the Italian Liberation Corps; the vehicles are camouflaged according to the typical pattern of the period, a sandy yellow background with brown and green spots, and the second car is fitted with "Libia" type tires (Pignato).

▲ A CV33 tank captured and used by Yugoslav partisans after 8 September in Dalmatia, probably in Split. The vehicle retains its original coloring and identification marks and is devoid of machine guns, perhaps removed by the Italian crew to sabotage it and render it harmless.

▼ In Croatia, especially in Dalmatia, the Yugoslav partisans took possession of many Italian tanks, such as this L6 / 40, probably captured in a cavalry unit. On the wagon there is still the plate of the Royal Army and the partisan who proudly mounts the guard wears Italian clothing and equipment.

▲ Alfredo Di Dio, Lieutenant of the 1st Tank Infantry Regiment, joined the Resistance after 8 September with the battle name "Marco", becoming commander of the Valtoce partisan formation. During the retreat following the fall of the Ossola Republic, Di Dio fell into an ambush on 12 October 1944. The Gold Medal for Military Valor was awarded to his memory.

▲ The Second Lieutenant of the 4th Tank Regiment Raffaello Parri, standard bearer of the Regiment, photographed on March 3, 1944 in a policeman's uniform: some tankers of the 4th Regiment, in fact, after the clashes of September 1943, passed to the dependencies of the Police, which in Rome had of its own armored department. The Lieutenant, after having participated in the battle of Porta San Paolo, joined the Roman military clandestine formations (Parri).

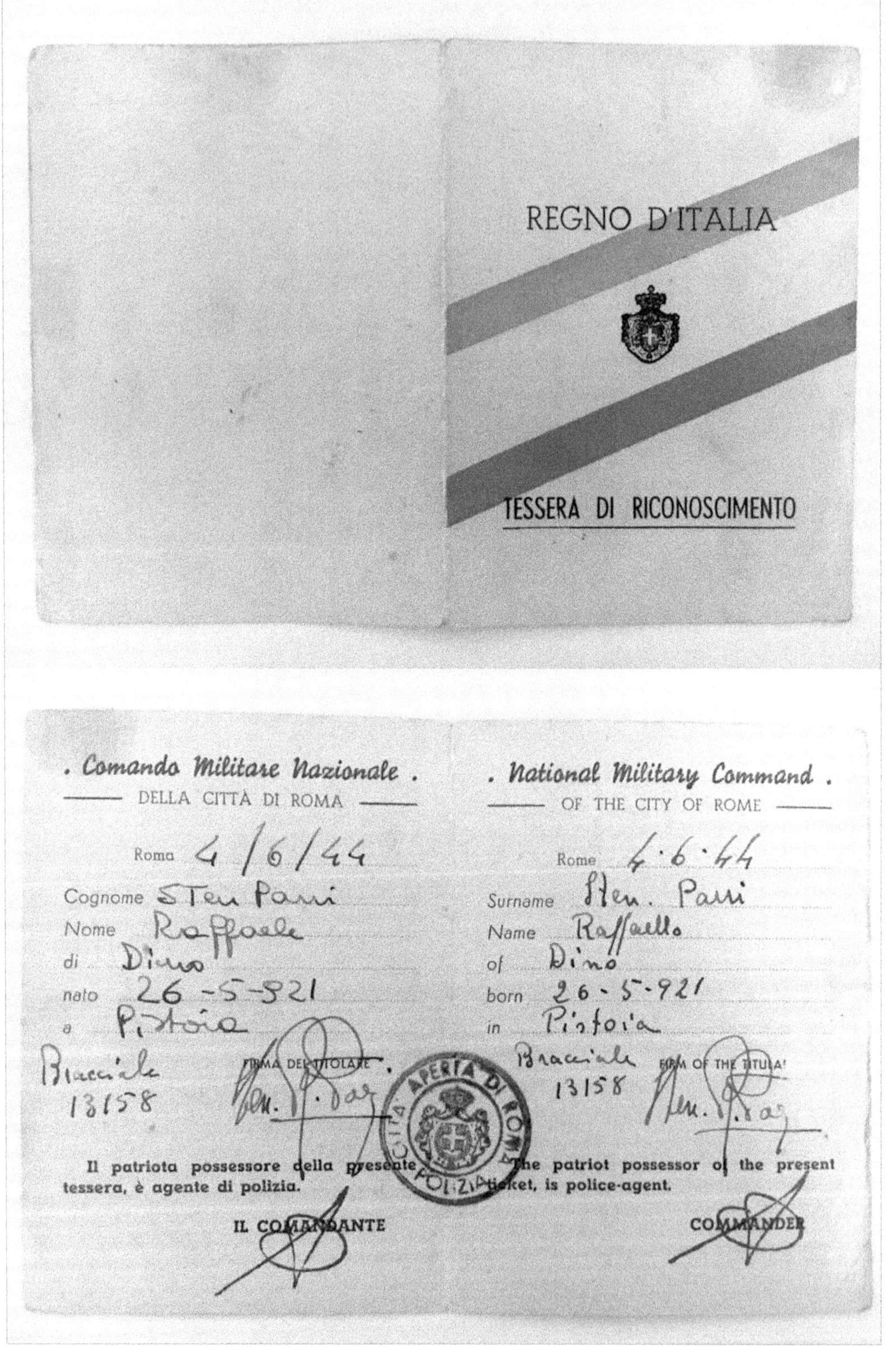

REGNO D'ITALIA

TESSERA DI RICONOSCIMENTO

. *Comando Militare Nazionale* .

DELLA CITTÀ DI ROMA

Roma 4/6/44

Cognome S.Ten Parri

Nome Raffaele

di Dino

nato 26-5-921

a Pistoia

Bracciale 13158

FIRMA DEL TITOLARE

Il patriota possessore della presente tessera, è agente di polizia.

IL COMANDANTE

. *National Military Command* .

OF THE CITY OF ROME

Rome 4.6.44

Surname Sten. Parri

Name Raffaello

of Dino

born 26-5-921

in Pistoia

Bracciale 13158

FIRM OF THE TITULA'

The patriot possessor of the present ticket, is police-agent.

COMMANDER

CITTÀ APERTA DI ROMA POLIZIA

▲ Front and back of the identity card issued to Tanker Lieutenant Raffaello Parri by the National Military Command of the City of Rome, which identified him as a police officer, belonging to the Resistance. On the card, in addition to the stamp of the Police of the "Open City" of Rome, the number of the bracelet used as an identification badge of the officer has been pinned (Parri)

BIBLIOGRAPHY

Books

- AA.VV., “Storia dei mezzi corazzati”, Fratelli Fabbri Editori, Milano 1976.
- AA.VV., “Soldati e Battaglie della Seconda Guerra Mondiale”, Hobby & Work Italiana Editrice, Bresso (MI), 1999.
- AA.VV., “Piombino Medaglia d’Oro - Una battaglia di verità e giustizia”, Comune di Piombino, 2008.
- Arena Nino, “R.S.I. – Forze Armate della Repubblica Sociale – La guerra in Italia – 1943”, Ermanno Albertelli Editore, Parma, 2002.
- Barba Selene, “La Resistenza dei militari italiani all’Estero – Francia e Corsica”, Rivista militare, Roma, 1995.
- Barlozzetti Ugo, Pirella Alberto, “Mezzi dell’Esercito italiano 1935 – 1945”, Editoriale Olimpia, Firenze, 1986.
- Benvenuti Bruno, Colonna Ugo, “Fronte Terra” volumi 1, 2/I, 2/II e 2/III, Edizioni Bizzarri, Roma 1974.
- Bonciani Carlo, “Squadrone F”, Vallecchi, Firenze, 1946.
- Capitani Mario, “La difesa di Roma – Cronistoria dal 25 luglio al 29 settembre 1943”, Edizioni Stem Mucchi, 1973.
- Cappellano Filippo, Pignato Nicola, “Gli autoveicoli da combattimento dell’Esercito Italiano”, volume I, S.M.E. – Ufficio Storico, Roma, 2002.
- Cappellano Filippo, Pignato Nicola, “Gli autoveicoli da combattimento dell’Esercito Italiano”, volume II, S.M.E. – Ufficio Storico, Roma, 2002.
- Cappellano Filippo, Pignato Nicola, “Il Regio Esercito alla vigilia dell’8 settembre 1943”, Ermanno Albertelli Editore Parma, 2003.
- Carloni Fabrizio, “L’occupazione italiana della Corsica – novembre 1942 – ottobre 1943”, Mursia, Milano, 2016.
- Carro Giuseppe, Grioni Daniele, “Fortini di Sardegna 1940-1943. Storia di un patrimonio da salvaguardare e valorizzare”, Grafica del Parteolla, Dolianova (CA), 2014.
- Cataldi Umberto, Di Nardo Roberto, “La difesa di Roma e i Granatieri di Sardegna nel settembre 1943”, Stato Maggiore dell’ Esercito, Roma, 1993.
- Ceva Lucio, Curami Andrea, “La meccanizzazione dell’Esercito fino al 1943”, S.M.E – Ufficio Storico, Roma, 1989.
- Commissione Italiana di Storia Militare, “La partecipazione delle Forze Armate alla Guerra di Liberazione e di Resistenza – 8 settembre 1943 8 maggio 1945”, Ente Editoriale per l’Anna dei Carabinieri, Roma, 2003.
- Corbatti Sergio, Nava Marco, “Come il diamante”, Laran Editions, Bruxelles, 2008.
- Crippa Paolo, “I Reparti Corazzati della Repubblica Sociale Italiana 1943 -1945”, Marvia Edizioni, Voghera (PV), 2006.
- Crippa Paolo, “I mezzi corazzati italiani della Guerra Civile 43- 45”, Mattioli 1885, Fidenza (PR), 2015.
- Crippa Paolo, Manes Luigi, “Italia 43-45 - I mezzi delle Unità cobelligeranti”, Mattioli 1885, Fidenza (PR), 2018.
- Crippa Paolo, “I Carristi di Mussolini - Il gruppo corazzato “Leonessa” dalla M.V.S.N. alla R.S.I.”, Soldiershop, Zanica (BG), 2019.
- Crippa Paolo, Cucut Carlo, “I reparti corazzati italiani nei Balcani 1941-1945”, Soldiershop, Zanica (BG), 2019.

- Crociani Piero, "La Polizia dell'Africa Italiana (1937-1945)" Ufficio Storico della Polizia di Stato, Roma, 2009.
- Cucut Carlo, "Le Forze Armate della R.S.I. 1943 - 1945 - Forze di terra", G.M.T., Trento, 2005.
- D'Agostini Lorenzo, Forti Roberto, "Il sole è sorto a Roma", A.N.P.I., Roma, 1965.
- De Lorenzis Ugo, "Dal primo all'ultimo giorno. Ricordi di guerra 1939 - 1945", Longanesi, Milano, 1971.
- Di Giusto Stefano, "Il Gruppo Corazzato San Giusto dal Regio Esercito alla R.S.I. 1934 - 1945", Laran Éditions, Bruxelles, 2008.
- Finazzer Enrico, Caretta Luigi, "Le camionette del Regio Esercito", G.M.T., Trento, 2020.
- Fracassi Claudio, "La battaglia di Roma 1943. I giorni della passione sotto l'occupazione nazista", Mur
- Franceschini Luigi, "50 anni dopo", Associazione Nazionale Granatieri di Sardegna, 1993.
- Girlando Raffaele, "PAI - Polizia dell'Africa Italiana", Italia Editrice, Campobasso, 1996.
- Giusti Maria Teresa, Rossi Aga, "Una guerra a parte. I militari italiani nei Balcani, 1940-1945", Il Mulino, Bologna, 2017.
- Guerrieri Valerio, "Ricordo di Piombino 1899 - 1940", Bandecchi & Vivaldi, Pontedera (PI), 1994.
- Guerrieri Valerio, "Ricordo di Piombino 1944 - 1980", Bandecchi & Vivaldi, Pontedera (PI), 1994.
- Guglielmi Daniele, "Italian Armour in German Service 1944 - 1945", Mattioli 1885, Parma, 2005.
- Guglielmi Daniele, Tallillo Andrea, Tallillo Antonio, "Carro L3. Carri veloci, carri leggeri, derivati", GMT, Trento, 2004.
- Guglielmi Daniele, Tallillo Andrea, Tallillo Antonio, "Carro L6 - Carri leggeri, semoventi, derivati", seconda edizione, GMT, Trento, 2019.
- Guglielmi Daniele, Tallillo Andrea, Tallillo Antonio, "Carro M. Carri medi M11/39, M13/40, M14/41, M15/42, semoventi e altri derivati", GMT, Trento, 2010.
- Guglielmi Daniele, Tallillo Andrea, Tallillo Antonio, "Carro M. Carri medi M11/39, M13/40, M14/41, M15/42, semoventi e altri derivati", volume 2, GMT, Trento, 2012.
- Masacci Luca, "I veicoli corazzati italiani 1940 - 1943: album fotografico", Mattioli 1885, Fidenza (PR), 2013.
- Mattesini Francesco, "I combattimenti di Monterosi, lago di Bracciano, Monterotondo e Porta San Paolo", Edito in proprio, Roma, 2020.
- Marzilli Marco, Mori Alessandra, "Roma 1943-1944 ieri & oggi", H.E.-Herald Editore, Roma, 2007.
- Mei Bruno, "I Lancieri di Montebello alla difesa di Roma 8-10 Settembre 1943", Edizioni Corporazione Arti Grafiche, Roma, 1981.

- Meleca Vincenzo, “I carri armati poco conosciuti del Regio Esercito. Prototipi, piccole serie e carri esteri”, Associazione Culturale TraccePerLaMeta, Sesto Calende (VA), 2015.
- Monelli Paolo, “Roma 1943”, Giulio Einaudi Editore, Torino, 2020.
- Pafi Benedetto, Benvenuti Bruno, “Roma in Guerra - immagini inedite settembre 1943-giugno 1944”, Edizioni Oberdan, Roma, 1985.
- Papò Paolo Emilio, “I mezzi corazzati italiani. I primi quarant’anni”, IBN Editore, Roma, 2011.
- Papò Paolo Emilio, “Armistizio!”, IBN Editore, Roma, 2020.
- Parri Maurizio, “Tracce di Cingolo”, A.N.C.I., Verona, 2016.
- Parri Maurizio e Bianchi Carlo, “A Nessuno Secondi, le ricompense al valor militare ai Carristi dal 1927 a oggi”, A.N.C.I., Roma, 2020.
- Parri Maurizio, “Tributo al 31° Reggimento Carri”, Soldiershop Editore, Zanica (BG), 2021.
- Pignato Nicola, “1912 – 1985 Dalla Libia al Libano”, Editrice Scorpione, Taranto, 1989.
- Pignato Nicola, “Motori!!! Le truppe corazzate italiane 1919 – 1994”, GMT, Trento, 1995.
- Pignato Nicola, “Italian Armored Vehicles of World War Two”, Squadron Signal Publications, USA, 2004.
- Pignato Nicola, “Italian Medium Tank in Action”, Squadron Signal Piblications, USA, 2001.
- Pignato Nicola, Cappella Filippo, “Insegne, uniformi, distintivi e tradizioni delle truppe corazzate italiane”, T&T Editore, Dogana (San Marino), 2005.
- Pignato Nicola, “Un secolo di autoblindate in Italia”, Mattioli 1885, Fidenza (PR), 2008.
- Pisanò Giorgio, “Storia della Guerra Civile in Italia”, Edizioni F.P.E., Milano, 1965.
- Predoević Dinko, Dimitrijević Bojan, “Oklopne postrojbe Sila Osovine na jugoistoku Europe u Drugome svjetskom ratu”, Despot Infinitus d.o.o., Zagabria (Croazia), 2015.
- Ratti Italo Franco, “Con la Centauro, con la Monterosa”, memorie edite in proprio.
- Riccio Ralph A., “Italian tanks and combat vehicles of World War II”, Mattioli 1885, Fidenza (PR), 2010.
- Schipsi Domenico, “L’occupazione italiana dei territori metropolitani francesi 1940 – 1943”, Ufficio Storico dello Stato Maggiore dell’Esercito, Roma, 2007.
- Solinas Gioachino, “I Granatieri di Sardegna nella difesa di Roma del settembre ‘43”, Gallizzi Editore, Sassari, 1968.
- Tognarini Ivano, Panicucci Massimo, “La battaglia di Piombino”, ESI, Napoli, 1999.
- Tognarini Ivano, “Documentazione per la Medaglia d’Oro”, Comune di Piombino (LI).
- Tullio Saverio, “La difesa di Roma 8-9-10 settembre 1942”, Associazione Militari In Congedo – Lazio, 2011.
- Tumiati Gaetano, “Morire per vivere : vita e lettere di Francesco Tumiati Medaglia d’Oro della Resistenza”, Corbo, Ferrara, 1995.
- Zangrandi Ruggero, “1943: 25 luglio – 8 settembre”, Feltrinelli Editore, Milano, 1964
- Zannoni Mario, “Parma 1943, 8 settembre”, Editrice PPS, Parma, 1997.

Articles

- Cappellano Filippo, “La Divisione Corazzata “M” poi “Centauro II”, in “Storia Militare” number 133 - october 2004.
- Degl’Innocenti Carlo, “La battaglia di Piombino”, in “L’Unità”, 2 september 1974.
- Dondoli Alessandro, “Piombino settembre 1943”, in “Storia Militare number 72, september 1999.
- Falessi Cesare, “Semoventi italiani derivati dall’M13: una famiglia di poco noti veicoli da combattimento”, in “Storia Modellismo” number 3, march 1980.
- Galantini Cesare, “La battaglia della Corsica”, in “Resistenza e antifascismo oggi”, number 2, april 2012.
- Pignato Nicola, “L’8 settembre a Parma ed il 433° carri M”, in “Storia Modellismo” number 9, september 1978.
- Pignato Nicola, “La “Difesa di Roma” - 1943”, in “Storia Modellismo” number 9, september 1978.
- Prunetti Alberto, “1943 – La rivolta”, in “Left”, 6 september 2019.
- Tocci Patrizio, “XIX Battaglione Carri M42” in Studio Storico Militari 1999, Ufficio Storico dello Stato Maggiore dell’Esercito, Roma, 2000.
- “P.A.I. - Roma, 4 giugno 1944”, in “Acta”, anni XXXII, number 1 (95), jannuary - march 2018.

Magazines

- “Il Carrista d’Italia”, magazine of the Associazione Nazionale Carristi d’Italia, various numbers.
- “Rivista Militare”, various numbers.
- “Storia Militare”, various numbers.
- “Bastie – La Ville magazine”, number 41, “70eme anniversaire de la Libération de la Corse – Septembre – Octobre 1943: la Ville se souvient”, novembre 2013, Bastia (Francia).

Other publications

- AA.VV., “L’Esercito Italiano nella guerra di Liberazione”, “Rivista Militare n°1, Stato Maggiore dell’Esercito - Ufficio Generale Promozione, Pubblicistica e Storia, Roma 2020.
- Graziano, “La vicenda di Silvio Gridelli, soldato aversano resistente a Porta San Paolo nel ‘43”, in “La Resistenza nel Sud - Le azioni spontanee partigiane”, Congresso internazionale di Caserta- Mignano Montelungo – San Pietro Infine- 21- 24 ottobre 2004, Caserta, 2005.
- Malvezzi Emanuela, Dondoli Alessandro, “La difesa costiera a Piombino nel secondo conflitto mondiale” catalog of the exibition “Le difese costiere a Piombino nei due conflitti mondiali”, 1998.
- “Relazione sul fatto d’arme svoltosi a Piombino nei giorni 10 e 11 settembre 1943 al quale ha preso parte il XIX° Battaglione Carri M/42(31° Reggim. Carrista) ed il suo comportamento dopo tale data”, Tenente Colonnello Angelo Falconi, Archivio dell’Ufficio Storico dello Stato Maggiore dell’Esercito, Roma (Raccolta relazioni – 8 settembre 1943, rep. N 1-11, busta 2121/D/7/7).

TITLES ALREADY PUBLISHING

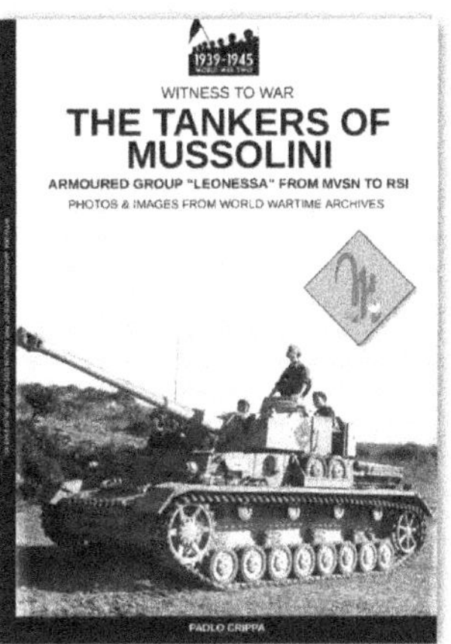

BOOKS TO COLLECT

www.ingramcontent.com/pod-product-compliance
Ingram Content Group UK Ltd.
Pitfield, Milton Keynes, MK11 3LW, UK
UKHW061827190726
13853UKWH00009B/2484

9 788893 277563